ARTIST SHAMAN
HEALER SAGE

*Timeless Wisdom, Practices, Ritual, and Ceremony
to Transform Your Life and Awaken Your Soul*

ALSO BY KATHERINE SKAGGS

PRODUCTS

Mythical Goddess Tarot Deck
78-card Tarot Deck with 136-page book
Author Sage Holloway, Artist Katherine Skaggs

Pocketful of Blessings
24-card Mini Oracle and Blessing Deck
Author and Artist Katherine Skaggs

Pocket-full of Goddesses
24-card Mini Oracle and Blessing Deck
Author Sage Holloway, Artist Katherine Skaggs

Altar Cards to Bless
Over 100 beautiful and inspiring 5x7 inch Altar Cards
Authors Katherine Skaggs and Sage Holloway, Artist Katherine Skaggs

Art
Original Art, Fine Art Prints, and Art Posters
to beautify and illuminate where you live, work, and play

SERVICES

Classes, Workshops, Online Courses
Coursework in-person and online in shamanism, the Divine
Feminine, intuitive painting, drum making, shamanic toolmaking,
soul mapping, divination and the tarot, and more

Soul Portraits
Connect to your true soul essence with Divine imagery
energy, and guidance. 16x20 inch painting on canvas with
video from live Zoom session - Shipped worldwide

Spirit Guide Paintings
Connect with your spirit guides, angels, ancestors, and totem
animals for guidance and healing. 16x20 inch painting on canvas
with video from live Zoom session - Shipped worldwide

Intuitive Tarot Readings
Empowering guidance for your questions, healing, and illumination.

Shamanic Healing and Spiritual Guidance Sessions
Intuitive, shamanic healing and spiritual guidance to
assist you in living more harmoniously

*Sign up for Katherine's newsletter, for educational articles and videos, free
readings and teachings, new products, and a multitude of offerings!*

www.katherineskaggs.com
www.youtube.com/user/katherineskaggs

ARTIST SHAMAN
HEALER SAGE

*Timeless Wisdom, Practices, Ritual, and Ceremony
to Transform Your Life and Awaken Your Soul*

KATHERINE SKAGGS

Star Chalice Sisters Publishing
Fort Collins, Colorado

A Katherine Skaggs Book

Artist Shaman Healer Sage

First Edition
Copyright © 2021 by Katherine Skaggs
Published and distributed in the United States by Star Chalice Sisters Publishing

Cover art by Katherine Skaggs, © 2021 Katherine Skaggs
Illustrations and cover design by Katherine Skaggs, © 2021 Katherine Skaggs
Book design and layout by Lori Beaty, www.clearlycreative.me

Learn more about the Artist Shaman Healer Sage Community Forum and other supportive products at www.ArtistShamanHealerSage.com

Library of Congress Cataloging-in-Publication Data

Skaggs, Katherine.
Artist Shaman Healer Sage - Timeless Wisdom, Practices, Ritual, and Ceremony to Transform Your Life and Awaken Your Soul / Katherine Skaggs. —1st edition.
ISBN 978-0-9821033-4-0 (paperback)
    1.) Shamanism 2.) Spiritual Self Help

        Library of Congress Control Number:
        2020922216

Tradepaper ISBN: 978-0-9821033-4-0
Digital ISBN: 978-0-9821033-5-7

1st Edition, April 2021

Printed in China

*With gratitude, I dedicate this book to my guides,
angels, and spirit helpers who have guided
me through many ups and downs in this Earth walk,
ultimately, returning me home to the love of Spirit.*

*I thank the Ancestors, the Star People, and Great Masters for
their love, wisdom, and dedication in assisting all of humanity
in its evolution and
initiation into greater love.*

*I'm also grateful to all my teachers, formal and informal, for
inspiring me to reach within myself,
that I might share with another.*

*In deep love and gratitude to all upon my path,
to my kin, and to Great Spirit.*

Katherine Skaggs

Community
Katherine Skaggs © 2008

Content

Huichol Meracame
Katherine Skaggs © 2010

Foreword

By Julie Loar

Interest in shamanism is exploding across the globe even though earlier religious fervor and cruel politics did their best to destroy this ancient way of knowing. The essential core of shamanism is the same in diverse cultures around the world, and the tradition dates back as far as 100,000 years. If we go back far enough it's likely that all of our human ancestors were indigenous tribal people with this knowledge at the heart of their cultures. Current research suggests we might even be pre-wired for our spiritual awakening; perhaps we carry a "recessive gene" that shamans understand. When the time is right and the methods are true a doorway opens into an alternate realm of perception.

Shamanism is a deep, rich well from which we can draw in our healing and learning. Katherine Skaggs reaches deeply into that well and triggers the opening of widened awareness, stepping fully into that other world of perception. Her wise and careful guidance activates expanded powers of mind. Artist Shaman Healer Sage is a powerful and practical guide for those who desire to step through this portal of wisdom with her as she sheds light on the path.

Katherine's book is a priceless compendium of the ancient wisdom of indigenous peoples, which is a timeless legacy. She teaches us how to work with all our relations--spirit animals, plant medicine, and crystals from the stone nation in a manner that is rich and approachable. We learn to work with guides and totems and she teaches us to call the directions and work with the sacred elements of fire, earth, air, and water. Her knowledge is shared in a way that makes performing ceremony and ritual with intention feel natural and graceful.

For myself, among the conflicting experiences of my now-abandoned Catholic upbringing, I have powerful memories of votive candles flickering in the dark church (fire and air), the pungent fragrance of frankincense (earth), and ritual blessing with sprinkles of holy water. These symbols had a profound impact on my young mind and were good training for the deeper spiritual work that would come later. My own experience with this ancient wisdom of worldwide shamanism began when I read Michael Harner's Way of the Shaman and subsequently had the opportunity in the late 1980s to attend his training, which was sponsored by the Foundation for Shamanic Studies. The shamanic training was life-changing, and I experienced a profound resonance with the practices that remain at the heart of my personal spiritual work.

When I moved to Colorado in 1997 I was drawn to Chimney Rock, which is now a national monument. The year before I arrived the Hopi had returned to dance at Chimney Rock after 900 years of absence. That event was a clear prophecy contained in their 10,000-year oral tradition that had been repeated in ceremony for centuries. Southwest Colorado had experienced years of drought, and so in their way, the Hopi danced and prayed for rain. In answer to their prayers the rains came during their dance, pouring healing waters on those who came to celebrate the return of Pueblo people to their ancestral land, forever changing the view of reality of those who came to observe. They sensed with visceral impact what is possible through intention and sacred ritual. The story of the dances at Chimney Rock is now part of the Hopi's ongoing oral tradition.

Indian dances became an annual event at Chimney Rock, bringing different tribes from the Four Corners. I volunteered and witnessed exquisite dances and met tribal people who changed my life. My most powerful experience was the day a Zuni sang and drummed a butterfly song. All was still as we sat around the Great Kiva and he began to sing and drum. As the song came to an end he was surrounded by dozens of butterflies, and there wasn't a dry eye in the circle. We were entranced, frozen by awe and humility, as butterflies fluttered around us like a benediction. The heart opens in such moments and our minds were filled with wonder and gratitude.

Artist Shaman Healer Sage is a treasure and a blessing. Katherine has gathered timeless wisdom from ancient wisdom keepers into a sacred bundle that she has shaped into the form of this wonderful book. Her wisdom is shared in clear language and easy to understand explanations. She has woven a sacred hoop with her simple but powerful teachings that can anchor us to earth and sky and help us navigate these long-expected times of challenge and transformation.

Mitakuye Oyasin!
Julie Loar, Author of Goddesses for Every Day

Rainbow Hope
Katherine Skaggs © 1997

Preface

The Omniscient Light of Great Spirit

Many, many moons ago, I began to search for spiritual meaning in life. The endeavor started not due to some great and lofty idea but a true need to heal my soul and find peace. I was always 'too sensitive' to the world around me. Through many challenges as a younger person, I traversed traditional pathways for my mental and emotional health. Ultimately, I was guided to the world of spirituality, metaphysics, dreams, and all things supernatural. Each time a piece of the spiritual world came into my awareness, I grabbed it like a hungry person at a feast!

Synchronicity was now in my favor as I leaned hard into this pathway of mystery and all things spiritual. All it took for me to go more deeply upon the path of experiential woo-woo learning was a profoundly accurate crystal ball reading at a psychic fair put on by the students of a metaphysical school. I remember listening to the woman giving this reading and thinking, "How in the world can she know these things?" As I spoke to her in bewilderment during the reading, she could see my curiosity as well as my wonderment as to how she knew these things about me. In the process, she told me, "You can learn to do this too." "What are you talking about? There is no way I can do this." I said out loud.

She continued to talk to me and tell me that I was born with these psychic abilities and that they are natural to each of us. I highly doubted this at the time. Yet, she went on to say that as we grow older, we begin to lose our natural, intuitive abilities when we are imprinted with the doubts and fears of our outer world and the people around us. When our parents tell us, "It was only a dream," and dismiss the power and meaning of our dreams, we begin to distrust our own guidance. When our school environment is focused only on intellect and reasoning, with little or no validation of our intuition, we begin to shut down our inner knowing. Little by little, our own Divine, intuitive nature dwindles as we look outward into a linear, ordinary world.

Though I was sure I did not have time, I signed up for the beginning series of metaphysics classes. I jumped in wholeheartedly, soaking in the teachings and religiously practicing the spiritual exercises. In a very short time, I became a teacher and went on to direct several schools within this nationwide metaphysical mystery school.

In the early 90s, the organization sent me to Colorado to teach and direct a school that was struggling to keep its doors open. Though I had a small number of students, I instantly became friends with one of my students, who told me she facilitated a shamanic journey process. I was immediately interested. At that time, I had yet to meet someone who did any shamanic work or knew anything about it.

I loved learning and was curious about shamanism. Yet, the real reason I wanted to experience this work was to gain clarity. At the time, I struggled with my position at the school and how things were being run. Things were out of harmony, and I needed to make a change but was afraid and didn't know where my spiritual life would go without this structure.

One afternoon I ventured to my new friend's home, had a chat and a cup of tea, and then went on to experience my first shamanic journey session. I went to her spare bedroom to lie down, where she guided me into a meditation and visualization process that she called a shamanic journey. Looking back, I can tell you it was nothing like what I experience today in my shamanic traditions, except that indeed I did journey out of my body and into the light.

I laid on a bed and closed my eyes, listening to her voice as my prompt to guide me within. She told me to imagine a hallway with doors. And I kid you not, I saw a hallway with doors as clearly as I can see the room I sit in now as I write to you. That was an amazing thing already, as I had been meditating, practicing remote viewing and astral projection for three years, and had never experienced anything so clearly in my life.

Next, she told me to choose a door to go through. I picked the door on my right. I opened it to see a beautiful garden. Again, I was amazed at its beauty, so clear and 'real.' I looked down and saw a fairy angel. She was beautiful and so very small. I thought, "I would just love to hug her." And with that thought, I shrank in size and gave her a hug! Then, I burst into light! The room was gone. The garden was gone. The physical world and all associated physical realities were gone. There was no time nor sense of physical space. I was in pure, omniscient, white light.

I was overcome by peace, bliss, and a fullness of love that I had never experienced on the physical plane of existence before. As I was in the reverie of this experience, I recognized the pure, omniscient consciousness of pure Divinity, i.e., God, Great Spirit, the Great Mystery, through me and all around me. I experienced an unexplainable knowing. I knew if I had a question that it would be answered. Yet there were no questions within this Divine, omniscient, white light. All was known. All was answered. Ultimately, I understood that the only answer to any question was love.

In earth-time, hours passed, from early afternoon to early evening. I had no awareness of time, or my body, or anything of the earthly world until suddenly I was pulled back into my body. When this happened, I looked at the clock and realized I had to go, as I was to teach in 15 minutes! As I got into my car and drove to school, I noticed neon auras glowing around everything. I am not sure how I taught anything that night with so much of my attention being drawn to my students' colorful auras. Though I had seen auras before, I had never seen anything so spectacular. I saw bright and vibrant, colorful energy glowing around my students, the plants, everything. This went on for three days.

Something inside me had changed with this experience. Two weeks later, I left my positions as teacher and director at the school, and all else that was causing conflict in my life. I was at peace with this ending. I was being led to a new dream, a new way of life, all with a sense of peace and love. Though I had no idea what was next, I was good. I was home in myself.

Since this experience in 1991, I have had many spectacular shamanic journeys and other mystical experiences with deep awareness and heavenly guidance, but nothing quite like this. I have asked my guides, "Why haven't I been able to get back to this place, as I experienced it then?" In response, my guides have let me know that this experience was a gift. It was to remind me of what I know and that I have been here before. They also wanted me to know that this 'place' lives within me at all times... I can touch upon it at any time when I still myself and put my attention on it. They tell me it requires no special talents; however, it does require my attention and keeping my heart and mind open.

They also tell me to remind you that this Great Mystery, this place of all-knowing, all-loving presence, lives within you too. I tell you this story now to encourage you upon your spiritual journey. Be curious, and you will align with this. Do your best as you embark upon the stories and teachings within this book to open your mind, as well as your heart. Do more than read the information given. Stop and try the practices given to help you clean away any illusion, hurt, fear, and all the imprints that limit you. You are returning home now. Learn to be still amidst the motion and the events around you. You are waking up.

Having this book in your hands now is one of the synchronicities upon your path. Being led here now, to read this story, is a perfect reflection of your soul's guidance.

Rites of Passage:
Awakening to the Love of Great Spirit

Eighteen years later, unexpectedly, I was led to the multi-cultural world and experiential pathway of shamanism. Suffering had once again nudged me forward on my spiritual path. Though I had already developed many in-depth spiritual practices, had grown, had healed, and had transformed, I apparently needed much more transformation.

This time a broken heart and sudden loss of relationship broke me open in need of healing. This pain was too familiar. I had been here before. Something was not right. Many tears, coupled with many prayers, opened my guidance once again. As I followed my intuition, one thing led to another until I found myself on a shamanic healing retreat with three international teachers of shamanism and

Kachina of the Stars
Katherine Skaggs © 2019

two Shipibo shamans from the jungles of Peru. Once again, I found myself exactly where I needed to be for my next cycle of healing and adventure of awakening to my true spiritual nature.

Before I knew it, I was enrolled in advanced shamanic teachings and ceremonial work. These shamanic teachings and practices were born of rich, multi-cultural, worldwide shamanic lineages — in particular teachings and practices from Native American, Siberian, Peruvian (from the Q'ero high in the Andes to the Shipibo shamans in the jungles of Peru), Huichols from Central Mexico, and various other Buddhist, Hindu and mystical traditions that aligned perfectly. Another healing cycle of shedding old patterns and imprints born of fear and trauma was upon me. I dove in once again.

Today, another fourteen years down my path, I do my best to live these teachings. I go into sacred ceremony and rituals often. Ceremony and ritual lead me to the place away from the linear world's workings, deeply inward to the mystical, and away from the everyday experience of mundane life. I need these spaces of stillness to find harmony and balance. As much as I do my best to be present to the mystery, and to consciously live a spiritual existence in every part of my life, I yearn for silence, quiet and complete stillness. These are the places outside of the linear world of time, the place of the North in the medicine wheel, where I journey within to rest, to fill up, and to be in touch with the vast inner workings of Spirit.

Divine Spark
Katherine Skaggs © 2005

Advice from the Ancestors

*C*ome home now! Come home to your hearts. Come home to *your inner light. Come home to the place where you perceive through the vibration of love and where you act only through the vibration of love. Drop all judgment and harshness. Foster compassion. First of all, foster these things for yourself, and then lovingly give them away. Then you will be home in yourself. Then you will be home in a world you have birthed through love. Only through love shall you act, for this is your directive.*
- Channeled message from the Ancestors
May 2020 through Katherine

Over the last months, I have taken many retreat spaces for ceremonial and journey work, both to assist others and to go deeply within for my own self. During these ceremonies, I have come in touch with the profound presence of the Ancient Ones, the Grandfathers and the Grandmothers, and the Star Nation. They have big voices, great wisdom, and very clear, direct guidance.

The channeled message above is clear, direct, and timely as our world undergoes great divide, political, and social chaos. The experiences of these times are more than I can describe in a sentence, yet I can say that it too often breaks the hearts and souls of most humans I know. Fear lingers among most of us, as we are being dismantled of our past into an unknown future. As the old dies before our very eyes and we grasp to hold on, we are being called to let go and to wake up. We are being called to focus our eyes and our hearts on the truth of a greater Divine reality emerging. Our souls call us to consciously choose love, no matter how challenging that is to do. This is the only way we will fashion our futures in a more harmonious, heart-centered way.

Great Spirit, expressing through the wisdom of the Ancient Ones, reminds us where home is. Home is within! It is infinite, timeless, and eternal. It lives in your heart and soul. It is here now. Do not be distracted by the hatred of those who are unconscious. Go to love. Keep your focus on what is important, what is 'right,' what is 'true,' and what is 'love,' for your soul is in an initiation for awakening. The only way to truly awaken is to learn what love is and then to love fiercely, stepping away from anger, hate, judgment, and all the emotions and beliefs born of separation, fear, and trauma.

Work with the various practices throughout these teachings in this book, and you will begin to walk the path of love. Learn to clean, and purify yourself on all levels. Then you can fill yourself with the love of the Creator. This is the energy represented in the beauty of your natural world, and in the eyes of each soul that you meet. If only you will look deeply into the eyes and soul of another, you will find the spark of the Creator within other, as well as within self.

Create sanctuary spaces for yourself, so you may find what true harmony is. Focus through gratitude, prayer, and ritual, and you will transform your very being, that you may be able to hold light and love for others as well.

Come home now! Come home to yourself, for you are Spirit. You are Divine. You are the child of the Creator. Come home to your heart. Do this for yourself, and you will do this for the healing of all of humanity.

Fox Shaman
Katherine Skaggs © 2017

INTRODUCTION

Artist Shaman Healer Sage is a foundational shamanic guide for igniting your creativity and passion as the conscious dreamer of your life. Great Spirit gives us many clues to living a life of joy, abundance, and harmony. However, as humans, we often walk around in the dark, confused as we chase linear goals, disguised and separate from our true nature as spirit. Artist Shaman Healer Sage shines a light upon the workings of Great Mystery, and to the eternal truth that we are spiritual beings having a human experience, souls upon a spiritually purpose-filled Earth walk. It also gives you timeless shamanic teachings, practices, and tools for living in balance, empowered to live in harmony and joy once again.

What if your life just got better? What if you had the tools and information for proceeding clearly in your life's adventure with the insights of a mystic, a shaman, and a sage? What if you knew and understood the energies of Creation—Universal Laws and Truths, and lived in alignment with them?

Are you excited to journey down your path of empowerment?

In general, shamanism is finding a resurgence today. These times are edgy, divisive, full of highs and lows, and challenging each of us to see more clearly. Our souls are being tested, tempered, and offered an evolutionary jump in consciousness through the intensity of these times. NOW is the time to wake up.

Indigenous peoples around the world have prophesied this time in human history. From the Hopi, Mayans, Hindu, Inca, and beyond, there are stories that tell of the ending of the Fourth World and birth of the Fifth World. These prophecies and myths tell of a great cycle of endings and beginnings that ultimately bring us through the present chaos into a new, golden age of beauty and awakening.

Imagine, too, that as soul, you chose these times and this place on Earth to incarnate for this experience! Woah! You set your spiritual GPS to arrive here and now to obtain these experiences so your soul would have a great expansion! Your soul's trajectory to become an awakened being, aware of yourself as a multi-dimensional being of light, experiencing as human, is on an ultimate and perfect schedule. Your soul's GPS is moving you through an incarnation as human to the multi-dimensional experience of homo luminous, often referred to as the New Human. This is the enlightened version of your true self, in body, here and now!

This is perhaps why ancient shamanic practices are as valid today as ever before; these practices assist you in moving from ordinary reality and linear time into the ability to navigate consciously between your spiritual self and your physical reality. You will not only navigate but move to a place of intentional creation and empowerment. Shamanic practices absolutely help you to interface between the invisible and visible worlds, between your expansive, unlimited soul, to your finite human experience and personality.

As you become quiet and peer objectively through this ordinary reality world, to experience the natural world, the world of Mother Nature and the Cosmos, you will begin to see and experience the supernatural world of Spirit, also known as the world of the Great Mystery. You will come to know through your direct experience that the world of the Divine exists within you, within each of us, and within all things.

This life has seemingly had a multitude of lows and highs, leading me ultimately to the mystical, shamanic path. I was called, just as are you are now. My soul's GPS sounded loudly, sending me in the direction my soul called for. The Universe answered my cries that were born of separation. No matter how far I had come, a part of me still cried out, to be united with my true self, to return home to my joy and happiness, and to return to peace and possibility. Notice now, you too are exactly where you need to be. You are being led. You are being supported and awakened in just the right timing.

As you read this book, notice how you feel in your body, in your emotions, and beyond your intellect. You are not only reading words. You are experiencing a frequency filled with the wisdom of the Ancestors and the consciousness of the Great Mystery. These words are beyond the one of Katherine. They are vibrational and born of the love of Great Spirit.

The 'inner yes' and the emotions you may be feeling are you 're-membering' who you are. Pay attention to the inner yeses that take place as you read and know something is familiar, or that you just know it is right. You have been drawn to these teachings by your soul's internal guidance system. Drink deeply. Take your time. Enjoy and practice what is given. And return home to your soul's true nature of unity and harmony with all life.

History of Shamanism from Around the World

'Shaman' is a word originally used by the Tungus tribe in Siberia and is translated as 'the one who sees,' 'the one who knows,' or 'the one who sees in the dark.' A shaman, whether female or male, always holds a special place within the tribal community. Their roles are as medicine women or men, as visionary and sage, spiritual guide, and psycho-pomp, to name a few. They are key leaders and advisors, always with a foot in both spiritual and physical worlds.

We have evidence as far back as the Paleolithic age (roughly 2.5 million years ago to 10,000 B.C.) showing shamanism as a spiritual tradition, with practices founded in mysticism, ceremony, and ritual. Practices of ecstatic dance, rhythmic clapping, and chanting of mythic words (mantras) demonstrate elements of achieving altered states of consciousness from which the shaman could see clearly.

Around the world, from past to present time, tribal and indigenous cultures use shamanic practices to live in harmony with Great Spirit through everyday life. These traditions are quickly penetrating western, modern-day cultures, as many are hungry for the spiritual answers and practices that will help them live life with greater meaning, purpose, peace, and harmony.

Regardless of the tribal origins, you will find that shamanic principles and truths are shared worldwide. They are understandings of basic universal principles: You are the dreamer of your reality;

everything has consciousness and soul; Spirit animates all matter; everything is energy; all is connected; things are not always as they appear; all is well no matter the appearance of things; as above, so below, as within, so without. All is Spirit.

These truths remind us that ALL life is to be respected, whether it be animals, birds, rivers, trees, mountains, humans, or stones. Life is an expression of the Great Mystery that links us all together.

Shamanic peoples also know that the visible world is a dream. 'This reality as we know it' is defined by our conscious, waking mind, and our physical senses, and is a limited reality. The invisible world of Spirit and its infinite, life-giving energy animates everything in the physical world. As we become more aware through our shamanic practices, we can perceive the Spirit world through meditation, trance, shamanic journey, contemplation, intuition, and psychic ability.

Our human-made and natural worlds, and the visible and the invisible worlds, must be given proper attention so we may achieve harmony and balance in our families, in our societies, and our environments. The shaman understands when there is a lack of health or balance in an individual, family, work, or culture, that there is an imbalance in the invisible world and the physical world. The invisible energies must be attended to and harmonized to bring balance to the physical experience.

The shaman acts as the messenger, guide, and weaver between these two worlds. She can move between the worlds through trance, journeying, and meditation. Through altered states, the shaman mends the fabric of the energetic distortions or wounds created by fear and trauma. This is how healing and balance are restored, returning the world to the natural order of balance, whether in an individual, a family, the community, land, home, and/or the greater cosmic order of all things.

The shaman is also considered a hollow bone, or hollow reed, for the workings of Spirit. She is a vessel for Spirit to flow through, unencumbered by the small self or ego. She is not the source of the energy that brings healing, but the architect of a vibrational healing space for the energy to return to wholeness. She is egoless and in service.

Shipibo Shaman Herlinda
Katherine Skaggs © 2013

The Emergence and Role of a Shaman within the Tribe

Traditionally a shaman is one chosen by Spirit to play a specific role within the tribal community. This path is not something one embarks on in a weekend class to attain a certificate saying he or she is a shaman. This is a path of the soul's destiny to become more luminous, conscious, and awake. Moving into the capacity of a shaman is an initiation into a higher frequency and a more luminous state of being. Dark nights of the soul, near-death experiences, illness, tragedy, loss, and shamanic dismemberment are often the experiences of deep soul initiations. Years of difficulty and severe experiences can be the tempering process required for the shaman to emerge into his or her role within the tribe.

Initiation and dismemberment of the small self, also known as the false personality, are the shamanic processes of stripping away of the outer ego. The false personality and former self are stripped completely of the skin, or outer expression, taking one completely down to the bones, so a new body and heightened awareness can form. Death of the old, outmoded self must take place for the wiser medicine man or woman to emerge. With this death and rebirth comes the embodiment of extraordinary healing abilities and the ability to travel between the Spirit world, the inner dimensions of consciousness, and the earth walk. A shaman also creates bonds with many spirit allies along the path, working in unison to bring harmony. She communicates easily with them, whether ancestors, animals, angels, plants, or minerals, invoking help, and guidance.

Once the initiation is complete, the shaman moves into service to the tribe and larger community, assisting in bringing harmony, health, and abundance to all.

Shamanism for Everyone:
Living Life as a Shamanic Practitioner

There was once an old and powerful Qigong master who was quite adept at his craft. He had been working with energy since a small child, learning from many famous Qigong masters over the span of his long life. One day one of his students came upon him in the woods where he was practicing. The student watched in wonderment for a long while as the Master gracefully held only one posture. The student then asked the Master what postures he should practice to also become a powerful Master of energy. The wise old man looked at the eager student, in no hurry to reply. After several minutes, he spoke without wasting a single word, telling the young student that over the years of many trainings, and having learned a vast number of postures from many wise masters, that now he only practiced the one. One was enough. He told the student, regardless of what he chose, do his best. Master your breath, master your focus, relax fully mentally and physically, be in sync with all around you and within. That is all.

Shamanism is a pathway of experience and direct revelation. Even if you were not born into a shamanic culture and tribe, shamanic practices can be adopted and used by anyone, anytime, anywhere. These practices and principles reveal the sacred within all life. Regardless of your faith or religion, shamanism can enhance your life experience.

Relax, breathe, and learn the basics as you endeavor upon your shamanic path. See what practices and teachings call to you. When you come upon a teaching or practice that speaks to you, stop, take it in, then try it. Use them on purpose and with intention. Start with a few things. Do your best. Journal your experiences as you go along. This helps you soak in your experience and honor your emerging shamanic awareness. Notice the small things, then build on them. Then blend your practices into every aspect of your life until every part of life is your practice.

Then practice, practice, practice. A shamanic practitioner, a shaman or a mystic, practices daily… in every breath. She understands that life is a grand adventure, with many cycles, not an achievement or outcome. Life is the ceremony.

True wisdom and mastery are born of experience that comes through practice, practice, practice.

Great Mother Divine Child
Katherine Skaggs © 2008

SECTION 1

THE SHAMANIC PATH OF TRANSFORMATION

IS YOUR SOUL CALLING YOU NOW?

*C*reator said, *"I want to hide something from the humans until they are ready for it. It is the realization that they create their own reality."*

The eagle said, "Give it to me. I will take it to the moon."

Creator said, "No. One day they will go there and find it."

The salmon said, "I will bury it on the bottom of the ocean."

Creator said, "No. They will go there, too."

The buffalo said, "I will bury it on the Great Plains."

Creator said, "They will cut into the skin of the earth and find it even there."

Grandmother who lives in the breast of Mother Earth and has no physical eyes but sees with spiritual eyes said, "Put it inside of them."

And Creator said, "It is done."

~ Unknown Source

Owl and Crow Medicine Girl
Katherine Skaggs © 2017

Finding the hidden truth of the soul within the dream of life is the grand adventure. Fortunately, the Creator gave us clues, Universal Laws and Truths, mapping systems, signs, symbols, spirit helpers, and shamanic practices to assist us in finding our way home to our Divine selves, and to the experience of Oneness with the Creator.

The shamanic path offers ancient and timeless mapping systems to guide you on the soul's journey of awakening. Shamanic maps are often born of legends, myths, and stories, containing clues and spiritual teachings along the way. Within these stories, you will find universal truths and spiritual laws that are imperative to finding your way through the challenges of the earth walk - which is the sacred, spiritual quest of the soul to look within and to know who they truly are.

The shamanic path is one of experiential knowing. It is now time for you to know the wisdom and truth that lies within you that is born of the Creator. Follow these principles and practices, and you will begin to awaken your inner Artist, Shaman, Healer, Sage, empowered, aware, and full of light.

Shaman Soul Portrait
Katherine Skaggs © 2017

CHAPTER 1

SHAMANIC PRINCIPLES

GUIDELINES FOR NAVIGATING THE DREAM WE CALL LIFE

If we look at the path, we do not see the sky. We are earth people on a spiritual journey to the stars. Our quest, our earth walk, is to look within, to know who we are, to see that we are connected to all things, that there is no separation, only in the mind.

*~ **Native American, source unknown***

Within this dream we call life, there are shamanic principles and guidelines to help you live in harmony within the dream. These principles are universal, applying to anyone, anywhere, in any time frame. Shamanic peoples worldwide know and understand these spiritual, universal truths, even if these peoples have never met one another. I first came across these principles in my early spiritual studies when I was in my 20s, under the guise of metaphysics, Buddhism, and consciousness studies. The universality of these spiritual laws and truths reminds me that Great Spirit always provides a map for every soul to awaken into greater love and wisdom. Once you are ready, all is revealed.

You, the Soul, are the Dreamer of Your Reality

Imagine you are soul, and not the body you live in. Before this life, you sat with your guides, angels, and council and began to dream. You imagined what you would like to experience, to learn, and to enjoy, and discussed this at great depth before you chose this life! In this great council meeting, you began to weave agreements with other souls in the timeless space of Spirit World, the place where your soul resides before and after incarnation as human — the life between lives. This is how you began the dream of this life now.

You wove together the physical location of where you would be born, choosing the culture, time period, astrology, and all influences to craft the fabric of your beginning adventures. You chose your parents, who would offer you challenges and blessings, as well as a specific DNA patterning for your present life's journey. You chose your family members, your lovers and friends, and other souls who would offer pleasure as well as challenges to grow by. You chose a body, a gender, and particular patterns of possibility woven into that DNA for your adventure that also would offer you a great variety of experiences. You wove the dream of incarnation into the earthen world of ordinary reality, always supported by the invisible world of Spirit.

Within the dream, you fashioned a spiritual GPS within your own soul's heart spaces, always available to guide you through your dream spaces. This inner GPS is your beacon and homing device to help you return home to yourself, to your knowing, and to your soul's desires. Before you incarnated, you programmed it very specifically with your soul's desires and purpose for learning, creating, and experiencing. You also programmed your GPS to direct you to specific souls you determined to connect to in this life. Synchronicities and coincidences are the vibrational matches of your soul's calling, manifesting in form. Whether consciously or unconsciously, you are aware of your spiritual guidance system through your intuition, synchronicities, and inner reflections.

In this waking dream that you have created, you have choice and free will at all times. You are the writer and the director of the play. You can edit, change the scene, pull out actors, put in actors, and redesign at any time you desire. When you become aware of this, you can direct your dream with greater imagination and power for joy, pleasure, and happiness. You can better align with your soul's heart desires, honoring them and manifesting them into the dream reality of life.

Fairy Hummingbird
Katherine Skaggs © 2016

Everything in Your Dream is Alive

Spirit imbues life force and consciousness into every part of the dream.

When you look around your dream, can you perceive that everything is alive? Can you hear the plants, the mountains, and the animals singing and speaking to you? Can you sense their consciousness? Do you feel the healing energies the natural world is expressing now? Do you talk to your pets… and know they understand you? Do you talk to your plants… and watch them grow more beautiful?

Ordinary Reality and Non-Ordinary Reality

Grandmother Spider -
The Weaver of the Web of Life

*O*nce, before time existed, an ancient Divine Mother - Grandmother Spider, also known as the Weaver of the Web of Life, sat quietly in the Sky World. She awaited the awakening of the Great Cosmic Womb, the place of all Creation.

As the Great Cosmic Womb began to awaken, Grandmother Spider took a very deep breath and began to sing a weaving song of energy, connecting the stars and the Spirit Doorway through which all life is birthed. Color, light, and song danced through the Universe, connecting all from the invisible to the visible world. The web gave birth, and the creative process was born, giving life and the specific vibrations of sound and color to the dream of each spirit being coming to form. As Grandmother Spider sang, she helped souls weave their own specific lessons and experiences within the Dream of the earth walk. Within the Web of Life, Grandmother Spider connects us all as One in Spirit.

~ A Hopi Story, as well as many other
tribes of southwestern North America

Ordinary Reality is the physical, material world. Ordinary reality is linear, dualistic, physical, and timeline-based.

Non-Ordinary Reality is the invisible world or Spirit world. The non-ordinary reality world of Spirit exists without time and is infinite. The Spirit world is born of infinite potentiality and possibility. This high-frequency energy of Spirit is pure light, pure love, and pure wisdom.

This heavenly realm is the true home of the soul, where we exist in omniscient love and truth, unified and whole. The unseen world of Spirit animates and creates the visible, dream world of ordinary reality, connecting everything referred to as the Web of Life.

The story of Grandmother Spider reminds us that there is no separation between the invisible Spirit World and the visible, animated physical world. The visible world is simply the skin to the world of Spirit. Without Spirit, the physical world decays and vanishes.

Everything is Energy, Vibration, and Frequency

Energy and matter are the same. There is no separation between Spirit, energy, and matter, only varying vibrational rates. These variances in vibrational rates, or frequencies, are why it seems that you are separate from other things, such as plants, animals, other people, trees, and so on. Everything is vibrating at one rate or another, never resting.

Sami and Hucha Energy as Described by the Q'ero Indians

The Q'ero, a shamanic people descended from the Incas, high in the Andes of Peru, are a highly spiritual and devoted people. Their shamans work diligently through prayer and ritual to live in harmony with the world around them. They give prayers and offerings to the spirits of the land, the mountain spirits, and to all of nature. Harmony is achieved through the power of prayer, reciprocity, ritual, and practices in cleansing dense energy.

As masters of energy, they describe energy as neither good nor bad, as Sami or Hucha. Sami (prana, chi, ki, life-force) is light, high vibrational, life-giving, and of the natural world. Hucha is the human-made energy of fear and trauma, low frequency, and deadening.

They will also tell you that each of us is made of starlight and pure Sami. This is the energy that is the creative substance of the Universe. Science has caught up with these shamans' wisdom, finding that this light is stored within the DNA molecules of our nuclei and that it is a dynamic web of light constantly being released and reabsorbed by the DNA.

An important part of being vital, alive, and awake within this Earth dream is to be full of Sami and clean from the deadening energies of Hucha. The earth, the sun, the moon, the stars, the cosmos, and the natural world generate Sami, bringing the most powerful life-giving energy to us each time we engage in nature. Sami naturally cleans the lower, dense vibrations of fear, providing an effortless way to come into balance, simply going into nature.

Hucha is dense energy, slowing everything vibrationally, creating blocks, and stagnation in the energy flow. Left unattended, it ultimately creates distorted energy patterns in physical, emotional, and mental health, finances, relationships, and every corner of your life experience. Illness, lack, and life difficulties, drama, and chaos are the resulting experience. The good news is that you can clean this up once you are aware.

> The power of dreaming a good dream lies in what you put into the dream.

When you feel out of balance, your first step to change is to admit that you need to clean yourself up energetically, mentally, emotionally, and physically. Do your best to take responsibility for your perspective, your imaginations, your words, and your emotional reactions. This is foundational to your return to balance and harmony. The power of dreaming a good dream lies in what you put into the dream. What you give, what you speak, what you generate through actions and feelings, always returns to you. **Whatever you focus on expands.** Use your practices to become mindful and heart-centered as you can. Then focus your thoughts and intentions well through your speech and all actions.

When you are ready, take an honest inventory of the spiritual, mental, emotional, and physical imbalances, or Hucha, in your life experiences. Once you admit there are challenges and imbalances, you can begin to unwind and heal the experiences from which the pattern of Hucha arose. Attending to Hucha, such as anger, hatred, greed, judgment, jealousy, frustration, fear, lack, and resentment, is one of the initial, foundational steps toward keeping your energy filled with light and full of creative energy. Even the simplest of shamanic practices can assist you in clearing these destructive energies, returning to balance and vibrancy.

Ayni and the Power of Reciprocity -
Another Teaching on Energy by the Q'ero Indians

Ayni is another important Universal teaching on energy and the power of reciprocity from the Incan wisdom of the Q'ero Indians. I learned this teaching early on in my Christian upbringing from the great shaman Jesus: "As you give, so do you receive." The Q'ero will state it a little differently, in "As you give something, you are entitled to receive something back. And as you are given to, you have a responsibility to give back."

Ayni is the state of balance and equilibrium created through giving and receiving. Within this teaching, it is important to understand that as you give freely, the Universe will give back freely. If you give with attachment, rules, and limitations, the Universe will give back in like manner. This teaching encourages us to find beauty and gratitude in the world around us and to give back in like manner.

Powerful shamanic ceremonies and rituals embody the practices of Ayni, as do the attitudes of a faithful shaman or shamanic practitioner. Life is truly the sacred ceremony, where we have the opportunity, if not the duty, to give in reciprocity to our planet, the plants, the trees, the animals, the waters, the lands, the sky, and all other humans as a way to return all life to balance.

Your Thoughts, Beliefs, Emotions, Words, and Actions Create

Every thought, every emotion, every word, and every action are woven energies, creating patterns in your life, all with varying frequencies and vibrations. Understanding how you create through your thoughts and words are essential to dreaming a good dream. Love, compassion, and peace create more love, compassion, and peace. These are the harmonious energies that give life. Anger, hatred, and jealousy create more anger, hatred, and jealousy. These negative or low-frequency energies separate us from love, joy, peace, happiness, and belonging, causing a lack of harmony. If left unattended, soul loss, depression, and illness manifest.

Two Wolves - A Cherokee Legend

*A*n old Cherokee grandfather said to his grandson, who was angry at a friend who had done him an injustice, "Let me tell you a story. I, too, at times, have felt a great anger and hate for those who have taken too much, with no sorry for what they do."

"But hate wears you down and does not hurt your enemy. It is like taking poison and wishing your enemy would die. I have struggled with these feelings many times." He continued, "It is as if there are two wolves inside me. One is good and does not harm. He lives in harmony with all around him and does not take offense when no offense was intended. He will only fight when it is right to do so, and in the right way."

"But the other wolf, ah! He is full of anger. The littlest thing will set him into a fit of temper. He fights everyone, all the time, for no reason. He cannot think because his anger and hate are so great. It is helpless anger, for his anger will change nothing. Sometimes it is hard to live with these two wolves inside me, for both of them try to dominate my spirit."

The boy looked intently at his Grandfather's eyes and asked, "Which one wins, Grandfather?" The Grandfather smiled and quietly said, "The one I feed."

~ Well-known Cherokee Legend

All is Well, No Matter the Appearances of Things

If you are feeling truth and alignment with the teachings and principals stated so far, perhaps you can also embrace the Universal truth teaching that no matter how bad human life experience can be at times, that from the larger, spiritual point of view, "All is Well."

Good News, Bad News, Who Can Say?

A Chinese farmer gets a horse, which soon runs away. A neighbor says, "That's bad news." The farmer replies, "Good news, bad news, who can say?" The horse comes back and brings another horse with him. "Good news!" says the neighbor. "Good news, bad news, who can say?" says the farmer. The farmer gives the second horse to his son, who rides it, then is thrown and badly breaks his leg. "So sorry for your bad news," says the concerned neighbor. "Good news, bad news, who can say?" the farmer replies.

A week passes, and the emperor's men come and take every able-bodied young man to fight in a war. The farmer's son is spared. Good news, of course.

*~ **Taoist Parable***

Life is much more than the physical experiences we have of growing up, going to school, getting a vocation, making money, getting married, having kids, retiring only to later die. Life is the school of the soul, an adventure of experience, which offers learning and growth. On this earth walk, the soul has an opportunity to learn from each choice and each experience: What is it like to be male or female? What do certain time periods and locations teach? What is it like to be rich or poor, privileged, or not privileged? No matter how wonderful or how awful, every single experience offers spiritual opportunities to learn love, forgiveness, creativity, cooperation, self-responsibility, and unity of all life. Every part of the earth walk experience offers growth and learning to advance the soul's awareness and wisdom.

Since the soul essential falls asleep as it incarnates into the 3-D reality of human, there is a game 'hide and seek' where the soul is on a quest to remember that there is a larger reality than just the 3-D human world or ordinary reality. The human experience offers the potential to see, to sense, to feel, to hear, and to know there is life, Spirit, and consciousness within all of the physical world. As you begin to sense and know there is more than just the physical world, you begin to understand how much more there is than this reality. Then, you begin to grasp that perhaps you are indeed eternal and that this is just a chapter in the adventures of your soul's journeys that are endless. This is where you begin to awaken from the duality of 'terrible, horrible, no good, bad experiences' to a larger perspective of Spirit's love. You begin to understand at a deep level within yourself that has you have a Divine plan and purpose for your experiences.

A Dark Night of the Soul Experience

Many moons ago, before the internet was born, there was a young woman who had the fortune of creating and expanding a beautiful metaphysical shop and center. This store became very popular, attracting both a large local clientele and many out-of-staters who enjoyed shopping, getting readings, and taking classes. Over the course of the seven years of this shop, she grew and expanded this store three times, which was 'good' news. Over the years, this woman worked endlessly, never taking vacations, putting all of her passion, time, and money into this beloved community gathering place.

Several years into owning the store, the woman began to get guidance to travel and teach, ultimately expanding to public speaking. Yet, she could not imagine how to step away from managing her store. So, she toiled tirelessly at the task of running the store until one day she became exhausted, drained, and physically ill from all that was asked of her... both physically and energetically. Soon she could no longer manage her beautiful store, or really, her life. Finally, one day, she could not get out of bed she was so sick. This was her sacred journey into the Dark Night of the Soul — she lost everything... her health, her business, her finances, a relationship, and worst of all, hope.

Through the darkness the woman was forced to go within, to rest, to reflect, as everything once so vibrant and important was stripped away. Despite ill health and great suffering, she continued to pray, asking for answers, guidance, and healing. In time, she began to gain strength, support, and awareness once again. She healed as she rested. During this time, she began to realize why she got so very sick. She gave all to everyone else and not herself, creating an unhealthy imbalance.

She began to understand this imbalance was born of unconscious destructive patterns. So she began to rest, meditate, and return to her creative nature that fed her in other ways. Wisdom came in time, as did more balance, allowing her to find a new way, and to imagine differently than before.

Though she experienced a great deal of suffering at this time, her spiritual self was truly okay. The soul's plan was indeed unfolding, bringing much growth. The suffering was a red flag that there was something out of balance, a misalignment with the soul plan. Yet, the spiritual being was good beyond the human dream experience. Guides and angels were all around, doing their best to guide the woman beyond any lack of awareness, that she might find her way upon her soul's path that had higher purpose and understanding. Everything shifted, and she returned to her well-being and many new adventures.

As you wake up within the dream, you begin to experience and know that things in this ordinary reality world are finite, yet, the infinite is within every experience. There is a realization that perhaps there is a spiritual essence and design to life and its experiences. Wisdom and peace come when you can reflect upon your experience and ask, "What did I learn from this? What is the higher purpose?"

Learning to accept what is, and to be present, allows you to see Spirit in the experiences and come to know that your spirit and the spirit of all beings have a plan in the greater scheme of life. There is purpose, opportunity, and learning available in all things.

You have choice, and life is the school for awakening the wisdom, compassion, and peace within you. Releasing judgment and separation from your life experience returns you to the Oneness and spiritually uplifting truth that All is Well, no matter the appearances of things! This is the path of compassionate neutrality, rather than the experience of human duality.

You Are the Blessing!

Friend, whatever you do in life, do the very best you can with both your heart and mind. And if you do the best, the power of the Universe will come to your assistance if your heart and mind are in unity. When one sits in the Sacred Hoop of the People ,one must be responsible to Self and Other, because All of Creation is related. The hurt of one is the hurt of all. And the honor of one is the honor of all. And whatever we do affects everything in the Universe. If you truly join your heart and mind as One, then whatever you ask for, that's the way it's going to be.

~ Lakota Instructions for Living
passed down from White Buffalo Calf Woman

As we begin to recognize the light within ourselves, we begin to see and experience the light in others. And for some of us, as we see the light in others, we can then recognize the light within ourselves. This is the teaching of the Mirror of Life. What you see and experience in another, and in your outer world, is the reflection of what is within you. Cultivate compassion and unconditional love within yourself, and you will have compassion and unconditional love for others.

I remember when I heard that 'I was the blessing' for the first time. I couldn't believe my ears. For most of my life, I thought and felt that I had done something wrong. After all, I had been told this, imprinted with this my whole life. 'I was a sinner'; my religion regularly told me how horrible I was from the time I was very small! My parents believed this, as did their parents, as did many generations before me. I was told I was a 'bad girl' as part of my religious heritage from birth, yet no one ever told me that I was sacred or Divine.

Through a great deal of spiritual pursuit, metaphysical teachings and practices, and now many years of shamanic practices, I have come to understand these are all fearful lies, told to control rather than to empower. Do you also have similar wounds or imprints on being less than? Does your mother or father or grandparents carry these patterns? If so, it is time to unwind these wounds, for ourselves and our ancestors. You are a child of Spirit! You are a blessing. The great shaman Jesus taught, "You are the Way, the Truth, and the

Light." He even told us, "You will do things greater than me." Well, what does that mean?

In my journey, I have come to experience that each of us is Spirit, in varying expressions, playing a game of hide-and-seek. We are Divine Light, sparked into a great adventure of the earth walk. The very light within us is the blessing that animates our life and feeds the greater Web of Life that connects us all. As you give your light, your love, and your blessings to yourself and the world around you, the world flourishes. As you embody your true nature, aligned with love and wisdom, you bless the vastness of all life.

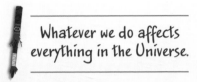

Whatever we do affects everything in the Universe.

I remember once when in a healing circle, I asked my teacher for a healing. I just knew something was out of order or wrong with me. This was a pattern for me, an imprint in my energy field and consciousness. As I sat in front of my teacher, I breathed deeply to help move the Hucha OUT of me. She put her hand on my heart and said, "STOP." I looked at her in bewilderment, "What do you mean?" I said. She said, "There is nothing to let go of. There is nothing wrong with you. Go sit down and let the energy in. Let it flow."

In amazement and disbelief, I returned to my seat. As I sat quietly, I felt a HUGE energy stream begin to come in through my crown into my body. This frightened me at first. I thought, "Oh no, what is this? Is this an alien energy?" Then, almost with a laugh, inwardly I heard, "Relax, it is you." Surprised, I realized this was my own soul coming into my body in a larger way than I had allowed or experienced. I was HUGE! My soul was expansive, and I was for the first time in my life, or at least since I could recall, coming home to myself. I was a very large light of consciousness, present in my body and life experience.

This was the beginning of my true realization that I had done nothing wrong, and that perhaps I was a blessed soul.

Bear Shaman Woman
Katherine Skaggs © 2019

CHAPTER 2

SHAMANIC TEACHINGS & PRACTICES

TO BEGIN YOUR JOURNEY

As you begin your journey into shamanism, become familiar with these basic teachings and practices to support your exploration of awakening the inner Artist, Shaman, Healer, Sage, as well as your work with the Medicine Wheel.

Shamanic Medicine

Shamanic medicine is an important concept to understand and embrace. For within every part of Creation is healing energy and medicine. Everything in the natural world has power, light, and wisdom. Each person, animal, bird, mountain, valley, and stream, each element, and expression of Spirit in heaven and on earth, has its own unique energy signature, or medicine that gives life. This shamanic medicine brings harmony and balance. Specifically, shamanic medicine brings healing, protection, vision, guidance, and specific powers needed for restoration.

Within your very being is your own powerful medicine. Your medicine is free of ego. It is humble yet full of power and wisdom. Your medicine is born of your gifts, your awareness, and the essence of Spirit that lives within you in your own unique expression.

Expressions of shamanic medicine typically come from the natural world, such as a stone or crystal; sacred tobacco or sacred corn; fur, teeth or bone from an animal ally; hair from your child or a beloved; a feather from a special bird ally. You will also find shamanic medicine imbued into sacred items, also known as power items, such as carvings, statuary, drawings, paintings, and sacred scrolls. These sacred items often depict a totem animal, elemental spirit, sacred symbols, prayer and blessings, sacred writings, a god, goddess, angel, or Divine being of light. These items exude shamanic medicine for an individual, a family, or a community, providing protection, healing, and guidance to bring balance and good fortune.

Shamanic medicine may be carried in a medicine bag, a medicine bundle (such as an Andean mesa), or medicine pouch. This medicine may also be worn as a talisman or sacred jewelry, carried in a pocket, placed on an altar, or in special places in your home or land.

Often these medicine items 'come' to the practitioner as a gift from another person, or a blessing from Spirit found upon a walk or another auspicious gifting process. You may also find your medicine in other places such as in a shop or at a trade show. You know it is for you, as you just can't walk away from it. It speaks to you in many ways. You feel more powerful with it. You also find that it has a sacred meaning for you.

When you are ready, your medicine will come to you. You cannot force it or make it happen. Relaxing into your heart always opens the gateway for your medicine and magic to appear. A feather will drop in front of you in the most unlikely place, or a stone will seemingly jump out at you upon a walk. It seems you cannot ignore it, are drawn to it, and are called to pick it up. Before you grab the feather or the stone to take home, always ask permission from Spirit. "Are you mine? Can I take you home with me?" Inquire with the spirit of this gift and Great Spirit. If you get a full-body answer of 'Yes,' then this is yours to take home.

Pay attention to synchronicities, and you will begin to see the medicine you have in your life already. Owls came to me in many forms for many years, in imagery, small statuary, and finally, the gift of an owl feather on my first shamanic adventure. A woman saw the medicine of owl in my heart and just knew this feather, which she had brought with her, was to be gifted to me. I have discovered over many years now that owl is indeed a powerful medicine ally for me.

Earth Mother Drum
Katherine Skaggs © 2019

Connect with Mother Nature and All of the Natural World

One of the most basic shamanic practices is to go into nature and work with all of the natural world. Shamans have known the power of nature since the beginning of humankind. Our so-called 'modern' culture is finally beginning to catch up with the value and healing benefits Mama Gaia brings when we spend time in her presence. Time magazine actually wrote an article on Forest Bathing in 2018 reminding us to step away from our electronic devices and into the fresh, clean air and high vibrations of the natural world to rejuvenate our mind, body, and soul.

Unplug from the tech world and venture into the woods, onto a trail, a beach, amid the trees, the through deserts, next to a pond, or into the mountains. Go to your backyard or the park and sit under a tree. Take a slow walk and begin to feel your body unwind as you feel the ground beneath you, see the plants and trees around you, hear the sound of the birds and the squirrels, and smell the fresh breeze blowing through your hair. Enjoy and drink in the experience. Imagine there is no place to go, no place to be. Be present to the healing energy offered by the vital life force of Mother Nature.

Grounding — Be Here Now

Grounding is a foundational shamanic practice of connecting to the energy of Mother Earth. It is an essential shamanic practice. When you connect to the earth in grounding practices, you literally are electrically connected to the planet and spiritually grounded into a loving system of support. Grounding, or earthing, is one of the most basic healing practices you can practice to restore your health and well-being.

If you are ungrounded, you usually have a hard time being present and available for the life you have to live. Your spirit is living outside of your body, and you are spaced out, tuned out, disconnected from your physical self, and most likely exhausted. This leaves room for foreign energies to take up residence in your physical body and energy field. These energies may be the external energies of others' thoughts and judgments, or they may be energetic parasites that 'hitchhike' and cause havoc. It is difficult to receive all the blessings.

Throughout this book, you will find many exercises to ground into Mother Earth and Father Sky. Try all of them out and see what you like the most. If you can't get outside in nature to feel your body sink into the earth, you can practice grounding through a simple grounding visualization given below, anywhere, and pretty much any time.

A Simple Grounding Visualization

~ Step into a quiet space, a meditation room, under a tree in your back yard, on your bed when you wake up or before you go to sleep at night.

~ Sit up with your spine straight, with your butt firmly planted upon Mother Earth (either physically or in your mind's eye).

~ Visualize putting on a pair of red sneakers on your feet, with magical magnetic qualities to connect you powerfully to the powers of Mother Earth deep within her center.

~ Drop a nice big, strong root as your grounding cord from the base of your spine, sinking it all the way to the center of the earth.

~ Inside of your root, place a copper cord to enhance your grounding ability. Imagine that it is anchored at your waist, then sinks down through the base of your spine and root down to the core of Mother Earth.

~ Say 'hello' to Mother Earth inwardly and with gratitude, connecting heart to heart as well.

~ Imagine there are two pathways of energy within your root system.

~ Visualize one pathway to release Hucha into Mother Earth, as she is happy to eat it, to transform it.

~ Visualize another pathway to receive Sami, to drink in the life force Mother Earth offers you.

~ Imagine this is a system of exchange and reciprocity through your connection.

~ Visualize the life force of Mother Earth coming up your grounding cord root system, upward through your spine, as if you are drinking in her nourishment from root to crown, filling your physical self, as well as all of your energy bodies.

~ Now, imagine a silver cord coming from your crown all the way into the heavens, connecting with the light of the Creator in the upper worlds.

~ As you connect, imagine once again a flood of light and life force coming from above to below, into your physical self and energy bodies, filling you once again.

~ Feel and sense the infinite flow of life-giving energy from Earth to Heaven and Heaven to Earth, with you as the central conduit.

~ Breathe. Fill. Open to the endless supply. Be present to the energy expansion and connection.

Once, when driving to Santa Fe in a bad winter snowstorm, though intently focused on staying safe while getting down the road, I dropped my grounding cord deep into the earth, as well as high into the heavens, anchoring my essence firmly in the present moment. I found deep support and comfort knowing I had my grounding cords firmly supporting me through my allies of above and below. I made it safely through the snowstorm to my destination.

Practice, practice, practice in private, sacred places, and in deep quiet and silence. Do this daily, and you will feel more vibrant, and full of life energy. You will also be more present and relaxed for all of your life experiences. Use this visualization when you need extra support being present, whether you are alone or in a crowd of people you don't know. This is an easy exercise that can take just a few moments or can be enjoyed as long as you like.

Smudging - The Power of Smoke to Clean

A Smudging Prayer

Into this smoke, I release all energies that no longer serve me, all negativity that surrounds me, and all fears that limit me. I welcome the light of love, kindness, and truth to illuminate me. So it is.

Our ancestors throughout time have wisely burned sage, palo santo, cedar, tobacco, frankincense, myrrh, copal, and numerous other plants and resins to clean their physical and energy bodies, their homes, lands, workspaces, and temples. Today, we may refer to these plant materials as incense or smudge depending on the form they are in. The act of burning the incense and dried plant materials is referred to as smudging.

The shamanic practice of smudging is as important today as it was in ancient times for performing energetic housekeeping on all levels. It is a sacred and prayerful practice, ceremoniously done. Each plant has its own energy, consciousness, and spirit. It is a conscious ally who is happy to assist the shamanic practitioner as its smoke carries the prayers to Great Spirit.

Incense and smudge are spiritual tools that can clean your auric energy field, as well as the physical body, your home space, your automobile, your workplace, and your land. Smudge and sacred smoke energetically clean low-frequency vibes, energetic cords, parasitic attachments, negativity, and emotional fallouts. Smudge releases negative ions, killing bacteria, viruses, and parasites.

Smudge daily if possible, to clean your body and energy field. Smudge before prayer and ritual and important events to set your space to a higher vibrational frequency. Use to clean away any conflicts or difficult situations you have experienced. Smudge and clean after you have been part of large events to restore the sanctity of your personal energy and that of your physical location. Use sacred smoke and smudging practices to put in good energy and blessings as well. Use it with intention to be in the flow in all circumstances. This is a basic mindfulness practice and not just a physical activity.

A Beginning Practice to Smudge or Burn Incense

A Sacred Practice and Ceremony - Use Clear Intention and Prayer

What is the purpose and energy of burning these plants today? Is it to clear, to uplift, to reset? Trust your intuition to choose your smudge wisely, as well as what you are learning about each plant and its powers.

Gather the following items at your favorite local or online metaphysical or shamanic shop. Wildcraft the plants if you live in an area where you can do so. Choose your smudge herbs and incense with clear intention.

~ **Smudge** - Choose any one or combination of the following: white sage (in bundle or loose); a palo santo stick; or a sage bundle mixed with other medicinal plants (such as white sage and cedar). Resins you may like to try are copal, frankincense, myrrh, and dragon's blood.

~ **A Shell or Large Ashtray** - You will also need a big ashtray or large shell to burn your smudge. To keep it from getting too hot, place a small amount of sand at the bottom.

~ **Charcoal Discs** - If you work with loose sage and resins like copal, you will also need to buy charcoal discs to burn the loose smudge upon.

~ **A Smudge Feather or Fan** - Use a smudge fan or feather to move the smoke where you want it to go.

Plant Spirit Medicines and their Spiritual Meaning

Every plant has a mission, gift, and purpose of assisting you, as well as has its own consciousness. You'll discover your favorite smudges as you begin to use various plants to clear and reset your space. I also suggest you try a variety along the way, as the plants have many gifts to support you. As you get to know the plants, you may want to use one plant instead of another to smudge. Or you may want to combine plants into a smudge blend.

~ **Sage** - Use to cleanse, bless, and bring healing to a person, objects, or place. Try white sage, desert sage, blue sage, or a mix of various sages to clear your space. Count on it to clean, purify, and bring protection.

~ **Palo Santo** - This is the 'Holy Wood' from the jungles of Peru. Burn to bring deep healing and clearing. Clears headaches, inflammation, emotional trauma, stress, colds, and much more.

~ **Sacred Tobacco** - Use with intention in sacred ceremonial ways, and to send your prayers to Spirit. Cleanses dense energies, removing trauma and Hucha. Use to set up protection. This ally should be honored, respected, and never inhaled.

~ **Frankincense** - An ancient resin used in ritual and ceremony to bring deep relaxation, inward focus, and wisdom. Many shamans use frankincense to call angels and other Divine beings for assistance.

~ **Cedar** - Slow burning and perfect for long smudging rituals. Cedar is known for cleaning, renewal, grounding, and protection.

~ **Dragon's Blood** - Use to clear bad energies, to bring protection, love, and empowerment.

~ **Pine** - Excellent for cleansing and protection. Very grounding. Known to bring prosperity and good health. In Druid lore, the pine tree symbolizes persistence, self-confidence, and moderation.

~ **Piñon Pine** - This plant spirit medicine brings the energy of Mother, fertility, abundance, and nourishment. Use when cleansing and purifying old ways of being, especially related to guilt or shame. Use to invoke unconditional love and nourishment after cleaning.

- **Sweetgrass** - Burn after clearing to bring in positivity and to restore the sweetness of life.
- **Copal** - This resin is well known to the Mayans and Aztecs in southern Mexico and has been used sacredly in offerings for centuries. It opens the crown, deepening your awareness to purity of thought, strengthens the auric body, and removes energy blocks. It helps with stress and alleviates depression. Use to purify your energy bodies, spaces, places, and objects.

Prepare Spiritually, Mentally, and Emotionally

- Set your intention and then move inward to a prayerful place, focused from the center of your heart.
- Graciously say "hello" and "thank you" to your plant spirit allies. Give them your prayers and intentions to clean your energy, as well as to fill up with energy before you light your smudge.
- Thank the Spirit of your plants for the work they have offered, as well as any other guides, angels, and helpers you have called in.

The Physical Activity of Smudging Yourself, Another, and any Space

- **Light the smudge** and let it burn until it catches, then blow out the flames until you have a nice billowing smoke.
- **Smoke your entire body** from crown to toe, front to back. Smoke the bottoms of the feet and the palms of the hands. Blow into your fingertips or hold your hands and fingertips above the smoke to bathe in the smoke. Generously smoke your auric field as well as your physical self, being mindful of getting 18-36" around your physical self.
- **When you feel clear**, clean, and centered, proceed to clean the space around you.
- **When smudging another person**, move through that person's aura in like manner. Have the person hold their arms out with hands open.

- ~ **Send the smoke** from the crown down through each chakra area, both front and back. Smudge the arms and the hands well.
- ~ **Within each hand is a minor chakra** that brings energy to the heart. Sending smoke into the hands and the heart helps to open the heart and centers that person more fully into their heart. This is an important awareness as you clean yourself or another.

Smudging Home, Work, and Sacred Spaces

Whole house smudges are an excellent way to clean and reset your space. This is another important practice to keep your environment pristine energetically, just as vacuuming and dusting are to clean your physical space.

- ~ **Prepare your smudge** in the same manner as you would to clear yourself or another, physically as well as spiritually.
- ~ **Move intentionally** through your home, directing the smoke throughout each room with a smudge feather or fan.
- ~ **Direct the smoke** into the corners of the room in particular, up and down the walls, and on all objects. (Energy gets stuck in the corners.)
- ~ **Smoke your altar** and ceremonial spaces as well.
- ~ **As you smudge**, sing, chant, and pray as you move through the space.
- ~ **Be mindful** of the love you put in as well as your desire to clear. Mindfulness and intention are the most important aspects of any smudging.

Suppose you work in a place where you can burn incense or smudge, proceed in the same manner as with your home. Leave incense or smudge burning in sacred spaces during meditation, prayer, and ceremonial work to increase the vibration and bring benefit.

Smoke your home or workspaces as needed. If there is ever an accident or argument or difficult event that you have experienced in your home or work, smudge as quickly as possible afterward to clear the effects of negative Hucha-filled experiences. Once you have cleared the space with smudge, burn sweetgrass or other smudges to add the sweetness back to your space, singing or speaking prayers of gratitude, love, blessings, joy, and harmony. Always fill back up with blessings once you have cleared yourself or any space.

Putting Out Your Smudge

Never use water to put your smudge out. Ideally, let your smudge and incense finish burning once lit.

If you have a smudge stick that needs to be put out, rub it into the abalone shell or ashtray until the embers have all fallen away. If it continues to burn, you can rub the end out into the dirt or sand. Make sure nothing is burning before you leave your smudge unattended.

Offerings of Smudge as a Blessing

The act of blessing is a powerful, alchemical practice that brings harmony, peace, and unity. Using sacred smudge, herbs, resins, and tobacco to bless raises consciousness through your intention and physical deed, creating beauty through their fragrance and high-frequency energies. Make sure to shift your focus to gratitude and blessings after cleaning your energy, whether personal, other, home, office, or land. Send prayers to your loved ones, to your community, and to the world at large.

Humanity needs acts of love and kindness as often as possible. Your personal practice of lighting incense and smudge, combined with heart-centered prayer, may be one of the easiest and most profound acts in doing so.

Smoke Baths for Deep Cleaning

There are times when we need a deeper cleaning than a general smudging may offer. Just as we do spring or fall clean-up of our homes, we too need to do regular deeper cleaning of our physical and energetic bodies. If you have had a recent fright, trauma, or emotional upset, or are working on healing ancestral patterns or long-term habits, addictions, and negative patterns, a smoke bath is suggested as part of your overall healing protocol.

Smoke baths clean the aura and psyche of the individual, releasing emotional, mental, and spiritual distortions at a deeper level.

Here's a simple way to experience a smoke bath:

~ Choose a location where you can enjoy lots of smoke in a sacred setting for healing!

~ Generously fill a shell or smudge container with any combination of sage, palo santo, sacred tobacco, dragon's blood, frankincense, or cedar.

~ Light to create a healthy, large fire. (Be safe!)

~ Allow your smudge to burn for some time until hot embers begin to form. When you blow it out, you should have large billows of smoke pouring out of the container.

~ Place this smoking smudge under a chair and sit over it, allowing the smoke to fully expand through your physical and energy bodies for deep cleaning. Sit as long as you can within the smoke cloud.

Peruvian Jungle Smoke Bath

This smoke bath is similar to the one above but has specific ingredients and a bit different process. This tradition is from the jungles of Peru and the Shipibo shamans I had the fortune of experiencing in 2018.

A smoke bath is for deep cleaning of all physical and energetic levels, and specifically supportive for psychological cleaning. It helps to clear away negative energies born of trauma and deep fright. These are the energies that cause psychic splits, personality disorders, anger, rage, and even schizophrenic energy patterns.

This smoke bath is best done outdoors or in a large space that is well ventilated.

~ You will need a large pile of palo santo, a bottle of Agua de Florida flower water, a small piece of alligator meat, a large smudge container/shell (or cast-iron skillet), and a blanket large enough to go over your entire body.

~ Dress minimally, in a bathing suit or your underwear, to expose as much skin as possible.

~ Place a generous pile of palo santo and dowse with Agua de Florida (flower water with alcohol and prayers in it) as a fire starter, then light it.

~ Let the palo santo burn until it turns into white-hot embers.

~ Add a 3-4" piece of alligator meat to the fire, allowing it to continue to burn.

~ Once the meat is also smoking hot, blow out the flames until it billows out of the container.

~ Stand directly in front of your smoke bath with your blanket over your back.

~ Hold your blanket up to your back and top of your head like a cape.

~ Take a deep breath, stand over the smoke, close your eyes. Create a tent with the smoke under you by bending over while pulling your blanket over your head and entire body.

~ Stay in the tented smoke as long as you can.

~ Pull the blanket back, step back, and catch your breath.

~ Once you have taken another deep breath, repeat this process as quickly as possible.

~ Repeat three or more times.

~ Use the remaining smoke bath to smudge your space if you like.

~ Place outside in a space where the smoke bath can burn down.

~ Offer the ashes to the earth, when there is no danger of fire, in gratitude for what is given, as well as an additional composting to the Earth Mother.

How Often Can I Do a Smoke Bath?

This is a question that often comes up once someone has experienced a smoke bath and finds it very beneficial. I suggest using it as needed, and always in a ceremonial way. Smoke baths are great to use in preparation for deeper spiritual work and when you feel you need a deep cleaning. I especially like doing the smoke baths when aligned with special astrological events, such as a full or new moon, solstice, or eclipse. They are excellent upgrades to general smudging and always offer a deep clearing when needed.

No Smoke Smudging -
The Medicine of Flower Water

Flower waters, essential oils, and their fragrances are an excellent option for working with smoke and fire. Plant fragrances and essential oils can be rubbed into your hands and breathed in deeply, placed onto acupressure points on your body, as well as diffused or sprayed into any space, through your auric field, and onto surfaces.

During the Black Plague in the 1300s, there is a story of four spice traders whose business was shut down due to the plague. When they ran out of money, they decided to loot the homes of the dead. The rest of the community were afraid to touch their bodies and belongings. Yet, the spice traders turned thieves believed they were safe as they rubbed vinegar, oils, and spices over their bodies and clothing. In the process of their thievery, they built a lucrative business, bartering stolen items for food and money. When the king found out what they were doing, he sent his constables to find and capture them, so he could get the recipe of what kept them safe. In exchange for immunity, the thieves shared their secret recipe with the king, which he immediately posted around the town. The secret recipe that kept them healthy despite the Black Plague was the combination of anti-microbial, anti-viral, and immune-building essential oils of clove, lemon, cinnamon, eucalyptus, and rosemary.

Flower Waters to Clear and to Bless

As with smudge and incense, your intentions and earnest heart-centeredness are most important. Use with the same intention and prayerfulness as with any smoke and smudge, both in your choice of sprays, as well as how and where to use. Your intent-filled prayers, your songs, and communion with the plant create the greatest healing magic. Give love and direction, always, when working with the consciousness and the organics of any plant spirit.

Here are a few of my favorite flower waters to work with:

~ **Peruvian Agua de Florida Water** - Cleans and clears. Dispels negative energies. Raises the vibration. Very good at cleaning deep, old, dense energy, fear, and trauma. Good to carry songs of protection and any directive for the highest good.

~ **Rose Water** - Brings in the rose magenta vibration of unconditional love. Excellent for the heart and relationships. (Rose has one the highest vibrations of essential oils on the planet.)

~ **Kananga Flower Water** - Dispels negative energies. Use to balance male and female energies. For cleansing, rituals of healing, and protection.

~ **Pusanga Flower Water** - Pusanga is known as a love potion in South America. It is for both physical and psychological support. It helps heal a broken heart, supporting love, health, career, and wealth.

~ **Tobacco Flower Water** - Use to clear difficult negative energies, fear, and trauma. Use any time you want to bring in the Spirit of Tobacco for cleaning, clearing, and resetting energy but can't use smoke. Use for protection prayers.

~ **Palo Santo Flower Water** - Great to clean, clear, and to raise the vibration.

~ **White Sage Flower Water** - Cleans, clears, resets, and protects, same as White Sage smudge.

Flower Water to Smudge Yourself, Another, and Any Space

~ Use your intention for clearing and blessing just as you would with the smoke smudge.

~ Pray, sing, and/or chant your prayers and intentions directly into the flower water container.

~ Pour a small amount of flower water into your palm.

~ Breathe it in deeply three times.

~ Then move your hands through your aura, from crown to toe, to disperse the energy of the prayers and flower water through your energy to raise its vibration.

~ Place your hands on your body in any areas that have pain or need healing. This intentionally sends the healing energy of the flower water into your physical self to clear and shift into balance again.

~ Pour more flower water into your hands, then sprinkle onto your altar, through your home, and where you need to shift energy.

~ Alternatively, put your flower water into a spray bottle. Spray into your aura, home, automobile, office, and land to disperse the healing effects of the flower water.

Create Your Own Flower Water Spray

Most shamans and medicine people gather their own medicines and create their own sprays. Here's an easy way to create your own flower water spray with fresh or dried flowers, as well as your favorite essential oils.

~ Purchase a small glass bottle with an atomizer spray top from your local health food store or online.

~ Add dried rose petals, sage, cedar, sweetgrass, or other plants of importance known to clean and to lift your energy. This can be a mix of flower and plant materials, or only one, depending on your intentions.

~ Optional, add 8 to 10 drops of your favorite essential oil(s) or oil blend.

~ Fill with distilled water or witch hazel.

~ Now, to invoke the shamanic magic, speak or sing a greeting to the spirit of your oils, say "hello!"

~ Thank the spirit(s) of your plant/flower medicines for their powers and for being your ally. Thank it for helping clear and clean your spaces, as well as expanding your prayers.

~ Now, sing or speak prayers of healing, love, wholeness, and blessings into your bottle of flower spray. Sing to your ally with love and gratitude. It is always good to be conscious of all your actions.

~ Cap the bottle tightly. Shake or swirl the liquid around for a few seconds to mix it all up. Your spray is now ready to go.

~ Spray in your office, cubicle, home, your own aura, desk, etc. It will be fresh as spring!

Essential Oils to Clear

Essential oils are high-frequency oil extracts from plants that are easy to purchase locally in natural food stores, spiritual shops, or on-line. Use similarly as the flower waters. Use frankincense, lavender, bergamot, or rose to calm yourself, clear your energy, and lighten your mood.

~ Put a few drops of your favorite essential oil (blended in a carrier oil) into the palms of your hands. Rub together and breathe in deeply. Place on your wrists, behind your ears, on your temples, and/or the back of your neck.

~ Place 25-30 drops into a spray bottle with witch hazel or distilled water to make a spritzer.

~ Add a sprig of dried flowers or herbs to finish up your spray. Spray in your home, auto, office, and around your energy field to lighten the energy.

~ Place several drops into a diffuser in any room you wish to clear and shift up.

The Power of Plant Baths and Love Baths

Plant baths and love baths are additional ways to work with the power of the plants. They clean and clear your energy with the power of water and plants instead of fire and smoke.

Plant baths are prepared with specific plants, chosen for their energy signatures, as well as spiritual and physical medicinal properties. These plant medicines are always gathered with prayerfulness, conscious intention, and mindfulness, always honoring the plants and asking their permission for use. The plant materials are then put into a large container, immersed in water, and then blessed, sung into, and consecrated with love.

Plant baths can be made to heal a specific ailment of the soul and body, to clear away energy, and to put in blessings. The possibilities are as endless as the many plant spirits and their medicines.

Make Your Own Plant Bath

Traditionally, plant baths are made from flowers and plant materials that are good for cleaning and purifying your physical and energy bodies, often in preparation for a ceremony or ritual. They also infuse you with high-frequency energy in the process. Since each plant has its own signature and "song" to bless you, it is good to learn about specific plant energies that are helpful to your intention and purpose. Plant baths can be made with a few plants (from three to five) or with many plants that give a symphony of fragrances, hues, tones, and flavors to bless and bring healing.

Begin by learning about local plants that grow in your area that you can source or gather easily. Each year I gather dandelions, roses, yarrow, daisies, sunflower, lemon balm, echinacea, mallow, catmint, and lamb's ear from my front and back yards to make plant baths. When I can get up to the foothills, I gather local sage, prickly pear cactus flowers, purslane, wild rose hips, and flowers, poppies, and other plants I am called to, even though I may not know their names.

If I don't have fresh or dried materials on hand in winter, I will turn to my local herb shop to obtain dried plants and herbs specific to my flower bath. I will also look into my cabinet for old herbal teas that may perfect for my plant bath.

Do your own research for any plant bath or smudge use, paying attention to the look of the plant, as well as what you can learn about that plant, what it is used for medicinally, as well as spiritually. The Doctrine of Signatures suggests that every plant has an energetic signature for a particular purpose. Its resemblance to human body parts, animals, or other objects will clarify the plant's relevance and its use. Names of plants are also often related to the plant's look or signature and can be giveaways to the purpose. For example, eyebright is used for eye infections; liverwort is used to treat the liver; toothwort is used for tooth ailments.

Always respect your plant allies by asking permission to pick their flowers and to work with their medicine. Be mindful in your gathering, honoring the spirit of the plant, and inviting it to be part of your plant bath. Notice which plants you are drawn to work with. Study their color, their physical presence, and their energetic medicine. Ask the plant to reveal its medicine and song to you. Be still, and you will hear their song! They absolutely love it when you will talk and sing to them, too.

Basic Plant Bath Recipe and Directions

This is a ceremony! Set your intention, be inward, and receive the blessings of the plants. Excellent before other rituals and ceremonies.

~ Think about your intention for creating a plant bath. Other than cleaning your energy, what are your intentions? Is it to prepare for a ritual? Is it to open your heart? Do you need support in bringing prosperity? Emotional and physical healing? As you connect with your intentions, ask what plants are most beneficial to support you in aligning with that intention. Get to know the plants and choose by both intellect and intuition. Pay attention and see what plants must be in your plant bath! They will tell you.

~ Get a large pot, bucket, or bowl to mix your plant bath materials and water.

~ Choose from any variety of flowers and plant materials that call you and work with your intentions. You can also use essential oils to add to the plant bath. As you choose, work with your gratitude and acknowledgment of each plant spirit for its powers and for being your ally. You are inviting it to bring its blessings to you and anyone you share your plant bath with. Be clear, be grateful, and give that plant a job to bring its blessings to your plant bath. I have provided suggestions with plant spiritual meanings below.

~ For every gallon of water, add 2-4 cups of fresh or dried plant materials. If you are guided to, add more. Trust your intuition as you put your plant bath together.

~ Place your fresh and/or dried flowers and plant materials into your pot, bowl, or bucket.

~ Source fresh water from a sacred stream, or a power place, if at all possible. Rivers, oceans, waterfalls, and spiritual power places, such as holy water, are excellent. Make your own holy water if you don't have water from any of these places by putting water in a container ahead of time, adding prayers and blessings into it, placing it outside in the sun and/or specific moon cycles.

~ Prayerfully add water to your plant materials. You can also add essential oils and other flower waters such as Agua de Florida water, rose water, and so on. Now is the time to put your prayers, gratitude, and intentions into the bath with all the heartfelt fervor you can muster!

~ Let your plant bath sit for six to eight hours (minimally), so the plants imbue the water with their song vibrations and energy medicines. Prepare early in the day and sit in the full sun of the day, gathering the solar medicine of the sun. Or leave out in the light of the full moon to soak in the lunar light.

~ Once the plants have soaked in the waters as described, you have a plant bath! Take your plant bath and put it into your shower area.

~ Take a shower.

~ Once you are physically cleaned and rinsed, use a cup to pour your plant bath over your head and all of your body. Be sure to scoop up the plant materials along with the water into the cup. Be generous in pouring as much plant bath over you as you desire. (Place a strainer over your drain if you are concerned about material going down your drain.)

~ Allow yourself to open-air dry with the plant materials on your head and body. Wrap a towel around you, but don't 'towel off.' Do the best possible to let these materials stay on you until they naturally fall off.

A few suggestions of flowers and herbs for your plant baths:

~ **Borage** - calms nerves; brings courage; grounds you into your heart.

~ **Catmint** - slows you down, moves you into meditative states, assists in dreams.

~ **Catnip** - stimulates visions and deeper inner journeys; brings peace and bliss.

~ **Chamomile** - calms and brings harmony.

~ **Lamb's Ear** - promotes kindness, tenderness, and gentleness.

~ **Iris** - brings the feeling of connectivity and nurturance through Divine love with the healing energies of Father Sky and Mother Earth; opens your channel between your root chakra and crown chakra; restores happiness.

~ **Mugwort** - opens the intuitive and psychic channels; assists in accessing sacred knowledge; use with yarrow to create a safe space.

~ **Opium Poppy** - assists in seeing from the perspective of the soul; helps with interconnectivity.

~ **Red Hollyhock** - brings joy, optimism, enthusiasm, humor, faith, and hope.

~ **Rose** - always provides the energies of unconditional love. Pink connects to ancestral love and appreciation; red provides more passionate, sensuous energies; yellow helps resolve conflict, bringing understanding and wisdom.

~ **Sage** - helps to clean low frequencies; brings higher consciousness, compassion, and understanding.

~ **Salvia** - deepens soul connection; promotes well-being, love, wisdom, knowledge, and union.

~ **Shasta Daisy** - (white with yellow center) calms overwhelm and brings one into focus, integrating many diverse ideas into the clarity of the whole picture.'

~ **Sunflower** - illuminates one's heart, expands personal power, promotes a healthy sense of self, helps one be more comfortable in their environment.

~ **Tobacco** - (Nicotine Rustica or pure tobacco with no additives) clears low frequency, fear, and trauma patterns, rigidity, addiction, blunted feelings, and hard edges; brings heart-centered inner peace; promotes physical and emotional well-being.

~ **Violet** - helps to lighten one up; connects one to Source and All That Is.

~ **Yarrow** - benevolence, purification, protection, healing, and cleansing.

The Love Bath

Love baths are a powerful variation on a plant bath. These may also be associated with a pusanga, known as a love potion, and magical perfume. This particular combination of plants has a beautiful and attractive smell. When combined with prayer and ritual, this plant medicine attracts good fortune, love, heart-healing, and success.

After deep cleaning and clearing, the blessings of love baths are offered to reset one deeply into their heart space, where love can be received, and blessings can be grounded into your spiritual, emotional, and physical experience.

Prepare your love bath just as you prepare your other plant bath, except with the use of specific plants known to open the heart, attract blessings, stimulate desire, and promote longing for love and happiness. The smell of these plants stimulates the emotions and awakens the senses. The power of a love bath penetrates your spirit and opens you to draw in love.

A few suggestions of flowers and herbs for your love baths:

- ~ **Honeysuckle** - for sweetness and nurturing.
- ~ **Jasmine** - arouses passion and desire.
- ~ **Passionflower** - for passion and attraction.
- ~ **Roses** - always synchronistic with love.
- ~ **Frankincense** - deepens your spirituality.
- ~ **Myrrh** - enhances spiritual attraction.
- ~ **Orange** - promotes joy.
- ~ **Salvia** - deepens soul connection, promoting well-being, love, wisdom, knowledge, and union.
- ~ **Sandalwood** - inspires love and bring relaxation
- ~ **Ylang Ylang** - awakens your sensuality.
- ~ **Vines and plants that are sticky** - for they draw together and attract. Ivy is a perfect example, as it winds itself around other plants, drawing them closer.

Anointing with Plant Bath or Love Bath

When you can't take full advantage of pouring a plant bath or love bath over your entire naked body, from crown to toe, you can simply anoint your crown chakra and all your energy centers with prayerfulness and intention. Place this medicine with care onto your physical body and into your energy bodies. Use your prayer and focus to direct it as desired. The plants are working for you now as your ally.

Prayer and Visualization to Clear Energy

The most powerful and discreet practice for clearing and shifting energy is through prayer and visualization. You can do this wherever you are through your intention, prayers to your allies, and your ability to imagine and visualize the shift into harmony.

~ The first thing to do is to center yourself into your heart. You can do this by simply putting your hand on your heart, taking several deep breaths. Breathe in and out a few times without making a lot of noise, but in a manner where you can move inward, even with your eyes open. Your attention is now in your heart.

~ As you breathe in and out, focus on thoughts and feelings of peace, unity, and unconditional love. You might even say a little prayer for the most wonderful, loving day possible.

~ Call the Spirit of Sage to you now, again with gratitude.

~ Imagine the smoke of Sage and all its powers going through your space wherever you are, encompassing the space and all the people around.

~ Imagine the energy in the room is easily shifting up in frequency. Imagine everyone is happy, harmonious, creative, and joyful.

~ As you practice this inwardly, feel the joy rising in your heart, your body, and in your energy field, expanding to every person. This becomes contagious and healing, always in the highest good for each person.

The Power of Prayer and Positive Focus

Whatever you focus on expands

When I began my spiritual path, one of the most profound Universal truths I came across was 'Whatever you focus on expands.' It reminded me constantly to be aware of my focus. And to gain greater mastery in shifting my focus to a more positive way of being and higher vibrational energy. Prayer helps shift one's focus to a higher perspective, cleaning away fear thoughts, doubt, anxiety, worry, and so much more.

Prayer is a sincere and humble act to petition, call upon, praise, and give gratitude to Spirit, or a spirit helper, through thought, word, song, dance, sacred actions, or postures. It is a conversation with the Divine. It is both active and receptive. Being inward and open to guidance is equally as important. A powerful prayer is the most intimate conversation with the Divine — genuine, and from the deepest, most heartfelt spaces. Shamans, mystics, and all wise ones turn to prayer as one of their greatest tools for transformation.

Your prayers are creative acts and invocations to call forth healing energy, bring balance, and bring assistance in the manner most needed. They are addressed to Great Spirit and your spirit allies who have great power to assist you. The focus of any prayer brings transformation. Whether your prayer is for clearing or manifestation, your prayer shifts your focus upwards to a higher, more Divine perspective. Consistent prayer develops humility, honesty, sincerity, courageous loving-kindness, sensitivity, and awareness. Aligning with the frequencies of these qualities are part of the journey to healing, wellness, wholeness, and harmony.

The ability to become still and focus from within the heart contributes to deep and powerful prayer. Centered, calm focus allows the thoughts, feelings, imagery, and words of the prayers to become strong and powerful. This is an essential quality that is attained through practice. Your walks in nature, walking a labyrinth, sitting at the altar in meditation, and prayer all contribute to the deepening of this ability.

Ritual and ceremony create a space for prayer to be deepened within the heart of the individual and the collective of the community. Individual ceremony and ritual fortify prayers, focusing their energy and making them powerful. Gathering a circle of individuals committed to prayer through ceremony and ritual exponentially strengthens the prayer, again fortifying the thought forms and petitions.

Genuine prayers deepen with time and practice. Fasting, retreating from the outer world in a vision quest or simple retreat, participating in a sweat lodge, and other ceremonial activities are all activities to deepen the power of the prayer.

Develop your practices of prayer by putting constant attention on gratitude and your connection to Spirit. Calling upon your allies with gratitude forges your relationships, helping you become conscious of their constant presence and desire to support you.

Enter into prayer mindfully, centered in your heart with gratitude. Pray gratefully with an earnest heart, opening to the love and gifts available to you. Visualize your prayers as not only heard but answered.

Then do your best to let go of specific outcomes. Open to the larger vision, and potential Spirit has for you and your life. Open to greater possibilities beyond what your human mind can grasp. Spirit works in the mystery, ultimately weaving a path of awakening as you surrender and trust in the inter-connectedness of life.

Who to Pray to?

Prayer can be directed to Great Spirit, God, Goddess, Allah, and all names you find for the Great Creator, your spirit guides, spirit allies, the elementals, the ancestors and helpers, honoring their powers and asking for their support in your life.

An example might be:

Great Spirit, thank you so much for all you give, for the abundance of good in my life, for the endless possibilities of experiences. I honor the light and the power of love to guide me. Help me to open to the guidance to know my path. Please help me to see and understand the signs and symbols you put in front of me. Help me to receive the blessings. Assist me in being inspired to create, to use my resources and gifts to bless this world and all my experiences. Please help me to wake up, to be fully me, to be harmonious, loving, and kind. Thank you for the vast love you provide and the reminders that are all around me. I appreciate the healing you constantly offer as I awaken on this path. May it be more beautiful than I can even imagine. Thank you!

Night Akbal
Katherine Skaggs © 2016

Cultivating a Prayer Practice

Take time daily to cultivate a prayer practice. It is an excellent way to begin your day before you go out into the world and engage others. Prayer can be done in any way…. seated, standing, dancing, singing, walking, lying in bed, etc.

A great and traditional way to pray is to sit at your altar, quiet and inward, with or without a journal. Light a candle. Put on some quiet, meditative music. Reflect upon your gratitude as well as your heart desires. Follow your breath, in and out.

Additionally, as long as you have your attention inward on your communication with the Divine, you can pray anywhere. On a morning walk, as you shower, or cook breakfast, or drive to work. There are no limitations as you communicate with the Divine.

Look for answers within as you walk, as well as in the signs all around you, the animals, the birds, the plant life, the terrain, and so forth. Be receptive once you have given gratitude and asked for support. Spirit will reflect its guidance in the outer world through symbolism as well as within your inner consciousness.

Prayer is great at any time of day, as you may well suspect. Intentionally beginning your morning through prayer can shift how you enter your day. Working with it as needed throughout the day is also excellent to keep your perspective high or to deal with situations that need a boost of energy. Prayer at the end of the day is the perfect bookend that completes the day. No matter how your day went, do your best to be grateful for your experiences, the growth given, and the possibilities that continue to come to you.

Altars and Altar Work
to Hold Sacred Space and Keep High Vibes

Creating altars filled with sacred items has always been natural to me. Even before I knew how to work an altar or to officially create one, I found myself making them everywhere in my home and workspace. On one table or another, I would have my spiritual chachkies, a vast array of special items gathered, and put in one place or another to create beauty. Quartz, obsidian, selenite, Herkimer diamonds, kyanite, lapis lazuli, and many other stones would find their way into special places in my home, along with statues and artwork of Buddha, Ganesha, Mother Mary, and Kuan Yin to accompany them. Altar cards of Jesus, Mary, Lakshmi, and White Buffalo Calf Woman also are placed about. Feathers found upon my walks, a river rock, a photo of my just-passed dog with a little of his hair; all sit in a special place on my altar in my ceremonial room. All of these special items, and so many more, adorn my house, from the bedroom to office to ceremonial space, making locational altars, as well as specific ones. Heck, my whole house is a sacred temple altar space!

Creating an altar is an important shamanic activity to focus the mind and heart on Spirit. Altars can be communal, public, or absolutely personal and tucked away from the curious minds of others.

An altar is born of intention as much as it is a physical endeavor of placing sacred items in a specific location, small or large. When created ceremoniously and in ritual, your altar is a place for sanctuary, prayer, meditation, and ritual. It is a place to hold your prayers and intentions and focus your love and connection to Spirit. An altar is a place of non-ordinary reality held within ordinary reality. Altars are for your spiritual mind and soul heart to merge with your personality. Whether communal or personal, altars help to anchor your focus on Spirit, love, faith, and possibility.

> An altar is a place of non-ordinary reality held within ordinary reality. Altars assist your spiritual mind and soul-heart to merge with your personality.

The Qer'o shamans of the Andes know an altar creates a portal to the heavenly realms. With prayers and attention, a portal is opened, and a column of light emanates from the altar into the heavens and down into the center of Mother Earth. This portal is called a canali. This canali acts as a gateway for angels, guides, and masters from the heavenly realms to come into ceremony and ritual, answering your prayers and bringing blessings from the supernatural worlds of Spirit.

Create Your Own Personal Altar

~ Set aside a place in your home that is private where you can set up your personal altar. It doesn't have to be large. It can be as small as your bedside table or even the drawer of your bedside table.

~ Clear it of all clutter.

~ Cover with a special cloth or covering that is beautiful and feels sacred to you. This will help set the space.

~ Choose some sacred items to place upon your altar that have special meaning and hold shamanic medicine for you. Each item should bring love, beauty, and honor to Spirit and integrate with your intentions. Examples might be:

- A statuette or photo of a spiritual master, animal totem, archangel, or ascended master.
- Photos of loved ones, family members, and ancestors.
- A crystal or crystals to bring energy or to clear and ground.
- Elemental offerings: A candle to represent the light of Spirit and the element of fire; a feather for the element of air, and messages from Spirit; holy water for the element of water; and sacred soil from any power spot or special land to represent the earth element.
- Flowers to bring beauty and sweetness. Very attractive to the spirit world.

~ Smudge all of your items before you place them on the altar. As you focus on each item, thank its spirit for the energy it brings to your altar and for the blessings it brings to you.

~ Use your intuition as to place your items. As you get to know the medicine wheel, you may want to consider this in your placements.

~ Smudge your entire altar with tobacco, sage, cedar, sweetgrass, or whatever combination of herbs you are called to use. Do this once it is set, and then regularly to keep it as clean energetically. Use the smudge to bless it as well as to clean it.

Altar Work

Your altar is the perfect place for prayer and meditation, reflection, shamanic journeywork, ceremony, and ritual. Take some time each day to go to your altar, putting your attention on Spirit through your heart, your prayers, your gratitude, and your intentions.

Several shamanic practices to use your altar:

~ **Prayers of possibility and manifestation**: "How good can it get today? What if my day goes better than anything I can imagine?"

~ **Prayers of gratitude**: "Thank you, Great Spirit, for all that you give, for all that I have, and for all the blessings to come."

~ **Prayers of release**: "Thank you Great Spirit, for your assistance in cleaning and clearing the Hucha, for cleaning my heart, my emotions, my thoughts, my body, my spirit, and all of my life for what no longer serves me."

~ **Prayers of forgiveness**: "Thank you Great Spirit for helping me to forgive those who have done harm toward me, knowingly or unknowingly, and for helping me to forgive myself for anything I have done, felt, said, intended, or held against myself or another that was not love."

~ **Prayers of blessing**: "Thank you Great Spirit for your powers to bless and to bring good fortune. Thank you for blessing me, my family, friends, and loved ones with good fortune, health, well-being, harmony, abundance, and peace. Thank you for bringing healing to humanity and Mother Earth right now. I invoke your power and presence in my personal world and in the world of all beings that they may receive these blessings and so much more than I can imagine."

~ Light a candle to represent the light of Spirit shining upon your prayers.

~ Burn incense or smudge to carry your prayers to Spirit.

~ Chant a mantra or sacred sounds to quiet the mind and connect to Spirit through the power of sound.

~ Play meditative/shamanic music to assist you in going inward to connect to your intuition and to Spirit. When you are quiet and focused, open to the messages and healing energies Spirit has for you.

~ Whether it be for a few minutes or a few hours, focus your love, gratitude, and attention to Great Spirit into your prayers and your ritual when you bring yourself to your altar. This small action starts the day on a positive note with your focus on potential and possibility for the day. It also is a nice way to complete the cycle of a day, as you recognize and honor all that you experienced and received in gratitude.

~ Come to your altar during the cycle of a day, to begin and to end, as well as on full and new moon cycles, equinox and solstice, birthdays and special celebrations, and for any ritual and ceremony.

The Shamanic Journey

The Shamanic Journey is the soul's ability to fly free from the tethers of the ordinary reality of the mind and body. It is where the soul moves through the doorway of the imagination into the world of Spirit, the place of non-ordinary reality. In this altered state, the soul is lucid and conscious of Great Spirit's symbol systems and messages.

> One of the most important practices for any shaman or shamanic practitioner is to gain a higher, spiritual perspective beyond their lower ego-based personality.

The shamanic journey brings answers, visions, and guidance. It is a place where lost soul fragments can be retrieved. It is also where you can clear away unwanted energies and patterns that distort the human experience. It is also an excellent practice to call forth assistance from spirit guides, allies, and helpers.

There are many forms of shamanic journeying that have been practiced for thousands of years, with each tradition varying their ways to attain this inner awareness. Some ways of entering the shamanic journey are through sound, such as repetitive drumming, rattling, clicking sticks, chanting, singing, crystal or singing bowls, and repeated mantras; ritual, prayer, and ceremony; plant medicine ceremonies; fasting; trance dance; vision quest; sitting and walking meditation; and shamanic, ritual art-making.

As you learn to journey, focus on your intention or question at hand. Always call in a spirit guide to assist you on your flight. And if you have a specific need, ask for an expert spirit guide to appear who will assist with that need or desire. Where you go and what you experience in your journey depends greatly on your intention and purpose for the journey. What do you want to know? Or to heal? Use your intention for your journey in as positive of a focus as possible. If you want to heal family trauma, make sure to ask to go to the place

Elk Journey Drum
Katherine Skaggs © 2016

of healing and wisdom for yourself, to gain clarity, and to align with healing. Remember, whatever you focus on expands. If you ask to understand the family trauma from its point of origin, you may have a difficult journey into the trauma, which can be very unpleasant.

The experience of the trauma is not where healing lives. Healing lives in a place of harmony that is outside of the trauma. So, focus your desire to heal into the place where the vibration of the healing exists.

Shamanic Allies and Spirit Helpers, Spirit Guides, Totems, Angels, Elementals and Ancestors

Once, before time began, as a bright soul light, before you were born into this life, you sat with your Spirit Council of 12. Together you began to dream of possibilities to set up your life circumstances based on your desires to learn and grow as a soul. Many of your guides, angels, and spirit animals sat with you in your dreaming, agreeing to support you in your creations and to remind you of who you truly are when you fall asleep within the dream. They knew that their task was a great and honorable endeavor, as was the dreaming of your soul into human form, which is one of the grandest and most amazing adventures of all. They all agreed, they were to be of service to you and your learning for the highest and best good in all ways.

Shamans are experts at working with their allies and spirit helpers, including ancestors, spirit guides, angels, elemental energies, fairies, animal totems, ascended masters, and so many more. Each ally carries its own energy signature and special medicine to assist you on your earth walk. Shamans get to know who these spirit helpers are and make 'friends' with these powerful beings as they rely heavily on them to assist them in all manner of their lives, from manifesting their dreams, clearing fear and trauma, to taking their prayers to Spirit. A good ally brings much protection and assistance, alleviating the shaman or shamanic practitioner from doing all the heavy lifting! Imagine that every ally has its own area of expertise and, when in good relationship, will do anything to support you.

To work best with your allies and spirit helpers, it is essential to know them through prayer, reflection, shamanic journey, and invocation. In the process, take time to build a deep and reciprocal relationship, full of trust, respect, honor, and gratitude.

Ancestors are the Ancient Ones, who have walked before you on this earth and are now in the Spirit World rather than in a body on earth. These are all your relations in the Spirit World. Yes, your parents, grandparents, and physical DNA lineage are, of course, your ancestors. Your ancestors are also those of your spiritual DNA lineage, those of your soul family. I also have found that spirit beings who have been in animal form can be one of your Ancestors, working from the Spirit World to assist you. One of my ancestors is my black Labrador, Lucky, who passed from his physical form in 2019. He has been a 'familiar' in many lifetimes, in various animal forms, and a few times in human form. I consider him an Ancient One and ancestor as he has been by my side since forever. I know he is a wise Zen master and assists me now as he has many times in other incarnations.

Your Spirit Guides. Before you were born into this life dream, you chose a team of five to seven spirit guides. You made agreements with these spirit guides to assist you in this life, for each one brings you its own expertise. They may appear to you as energy, male or female, human, animal, angelic, alien, etc. Guides and spirit beings are very creative and will get your attention if need be. They can even manifest in physical form as a blessing, such as an old man or woman in need, who then disappear as if they were never there. At transformative times in your life, you may get a new spirit guide, either adding to your team or replacing one of your guides. This is all agreed upon at higher levels of your soul as needed.

Angels, Ascended Masters, and Divine Beings of Light are powerful allies and spirit helpers to call upon. Imagine having great master allies and spirit helpers such as Jesus or Buddha, Mother Mary, Kuan Yin, Archangel Michael, Krishna, Ganesha, Kali, etc. as your spirit helpers! Whether a personal angel or a Great Master, there are an unlimited number of allies you can call upon to assist you. They are just waiting for you to request their help!

Animal Totems, Spirit Animals, and Power Animals. Spirit animals, animal totems, and power animals are well-known as shamanic allies and spirit helpers. Each animal carries its own medicine and expertise. Since we can physically see animals in our world, they are often among the first spirit helpers we begin to work with. Notice who comes into your world, whether on a walk or drive, where you see a particular bird or animal. Pay attention to man made references and imagery of animals, such as those represented on a billboard or in advertising. These spirit guides will flash their energy and image to you to get your attention when needed. Are you paying attention?

Plant Spirit Beings are also mighty spirit allies, expressing beauty through their physical appearance, as well as their individuated

Angel de La Luz, Nuevo la Vida
Katherine Skaggs © 2016

vibration and song. They are great at expressing specific light and song patterns for healing. If you are quiet and listen well, they will guide you to specific medicines for healing the physical body and the healing of the soul, the mind, and the emotions. Plant spirits are highly communicative and particularly love you to sing and speak to them from your heart.

Stone Spirit Beings are powerful allies born of the mineral kingdom, bringing consciousness through their own special vibrations and energetic structure and form. Many people are drawn to crystals and stones as they begin upon their spiritual path. A river rock, a mountain stone, and a crystal found in a metaphysical store have their own unique and amazing powers. Stone spirits easily communicate through their color, form, and energy. Both stone spirits and plant spirits are very good for assisting you in aligning your energy bodies and physical self.

Elementals, the Four Directions, Mother Earth, and Father Sky. The elemental energies: Earth, Air, Fire, and Water; and the seven directions of the Medicine Wheel: East, South, West, North, Father Sky, Mother Earth, and Great Spirit, are all conscious allies. They are helping spirits who have their own powers, gifts, and qualities. They are important allies to gain favor with as you deepen your shamanic practices.

The Artist, Shaman, Healer, Sage. Within your very being are many illuminated, archetypal powerhouse allies, such as the Artist, the Shaman, the Healer, and the Sage. Cultivating deep relationships with these allies and your inner Child, your inner Christ, your inner Clown, and others you may discover on this journey can expand how you see your vast spiritual essence and how you experience your huge spirit.

How to Cultivate Deep, Meaningful Relationships with Your Allies

Say, "Hello." Even if you aren't sure who you are allies are at the moment, center in your heart, connecting to your desire to know and connect to your spirit helpers, and say, "hello." Through your intention, focus, and desire, and the action of saying "hello," your allies and spirit helpers will respond. They get excited. They feel your desire to connect. And they begin to imagine how to answer you, so you know they are there.

Say, "Thank you." Now that you have their attention give them your gratitude. Say, "thank you!" Thank them for being your guides and helpers. Thank them for the powers they bring to you to support your earth and soul adventures. Even when you don't know who they are or what their gifts are, thank them for being here for you.

Give your allies an offering. Give your attention to your allies, and they will begin to return the attention to you. Your "hello" and your gratitude are your first offerings. Now add any additional gestures that you would like. Say a prayer. Offer sacred tobacco or cornmeal to your altar or a place on the earth in honor of your allies, either individually or collectively. Light a candle. Send sacred smoke. Your heart will know.

Be Curious. "Who are they? Where are they?" Be child-like and drop into curiosity to know your allies. Ask, "Who are you? Have I noticed you before? Would you show me a sign or symbol of who you are and what your powers are?" Repeatedly say hello, thank you, and give offerings. Then repeatedly look for signs and symbols in your world. What animal flew above you today? Did you find a penny on the ground? Did a U-Haul truck drive by with an animal on it that caught your attention? Does an owl itself, or the image of an owl, keep showing up and catching your attention?

Get to Know Your Allies' Special Powers and Gifts Then Acknowledge Them, Name Their Gifts

As you begin to recognize various allies who come to your awareness, get to know its special powers, medicines, and gifts. If owl has gotten your attention recently, observe its actions in the natural world to learn more about it. Or look it up in mythology, online, or in an animal totem book to know more about its shamanic medicines and spiritual meanings. Owl is the symbol of wisdom and is often seen as the one who brings death. Owl is the totem of the West in the medicine wheel and is very good at cleaning away fear and trauma while helping release old patterns.

Look around. There are messages everywhere, in many forms, to get your attention. Your allies and spirit helpers are constantly doing their best to let you know they are present.

Since I know these things about this spirit ally, I like to acknowledge them as part of my gratitude and prayers for my owl ally. My prayers and greetings with this spirit ally may go something like this: "Owl, thank you so much for being my spirit ally. Thank you for helping me to clear fear. Thank you for assisting me in cleaning up old patterns so that I may be harmonious and awake. I also appreciate your great wisdom, as I know you guide me to see through the illusions of this world. I need your assistance now, to …".

It is always an excellent idea to acknowledge the qualities and powers your spirit ally has. This honors them and calls upon these very powers to assist you in your life adventure. It also assists you in identifying which allies you might need at any particular time.

In some cases, you may not know what the expert gifts and powers of an ally are. You may just know that you have an ally who is present, and you would like to get to know them better. In that case, ask them to show you to communicate them to you. Ask them if you can call upon them for help in particular areas of your life. As you do so, be present and be patient, for they will find a way to show you how they can assist you.

And if for any reason you aren't sure who to call on when you need support, ask the expert guides, helpers, and angels to come. Ask for the most amazing Divine guidance and power to show up. Honor that they hear you and know your needs, then give them the gratitude and honor they deserve. Calm your mind and your spirit, and be open to receive.

Navigating the Road of Life
Shamanic Maps, Signs, Symbols, and Messages

*A*ll you need is the plan, the road map,
and the courage to press on to your destination.
~Earl Nightingale

The world of shamanism has many overlays and archetypal mapping systems. When you work with these symbol systems, you will understand that Spirit is always communicating with you, both internally and externally. Each mapping system provides a set of external symbols, when understood, that bring powerful messages and guidance from Spirit.

The Medicine Wheel

The Medicine Wheel, also known as the Sacred Hoop of Life, is a symbol system that teaches us about cycles from conception to birth, to adolescence and maturity, to death and rest. It shows us about flow and balance in our earth walk. It teaches us about the support given through the allies of each direction, Mother Earth, Father Sky, and Great Spirit. Get to know the Medicine Wheel and all of its components, as it will assist you in understanding the cycles you traverse, not only on a daily, seasonal and annual cycle but also on the cycles of your soul's experiences. This is one of the most important tools you can know in the shamanic mapping system.

Character Archetypes

Within every one of us lives a multitude of archetypal characters who assist us in navigating our world. Each archetype is an expression of an energy pattern. It has power, medicine, and consciousness. Each has qualities and specialized powers unique to that character.

You may naturally embody the energy of a warrior, a healer, a priest or priestess, an artisan, a scholar, or many other archetypal patterns. Each archetype offers powerful shamanic medicine to help you live life in harmony. It also offers shadow medicine filled with many learning opportunities. Each pattern you carry this life is part of your soul's mapping system of energies that you are working with to learn and grow. When you become aware of the archetypal patterns in your nature and soul's symbol system, you can work more consciously with it to be empowered and in balance.

Within these shamanic teachings, you will have the opportunity to explore the powerful archetypes of the Artist, Shaman, Healer, Sage. These archetypes are available to each of us as we awaken our higher consciousness. Intentionally engage the power of these archetypes to discover the healing power and creativity of your own soul's capacity. These are both powerful allies that live within you and within a larger universal mapping system.

Animal Totems, Plant Spirits, Stone Spirits, and All Things of the Natural World

Other mapping systems include the symbol systems and messages that come through animal totems, plant spirit medicines, stone spirits, and all things born of Spirit through the natural world. This includes the medicine of the stars, the planets, and the movement of the cosmos. Take time to learn about the energy and story of a totem or spirit animal. Include all animals, birds, insects, reptiles, and mythical creatures, when they show up in your life. Study

Owl Totem
Katherine Skaggs © 2002

how this ally showed itself to you through its actions and how this animal lives its life so you can understand what message it is trying to bring you in your life. Do the same for plants, crystals, and stones.

Archangels, Ascended Masters, Gods, and Goddesses, Heavenly Divine Beings of Light

Each angel, ascended master, and Divine Being of Light carries its own messages, energy signatures, and purpose. They, too, provide symbol systems to work with, just as animal totems and character archetypes do.

Day Dreams and Night Dreams

Learning the symbol language of dreams, also known as the 'language of the soul,' is an essential way to learn more about the soul's symbol systems. Your night dreams are a universal symbol system from your inner self, your subconscious, to your outer, waking conscious mind. Every night, whether you recall it or not, you have a dream or series of dreams that give you guidance on your everyday life.

Everyone in the dream is you, the dreamer. Everyone and everything in the dream reflect your state of consciousness, giving you a 24 to 72-hour feedback loop on your daily life and how you are creating it. This symbol system of night dreams can also be applied directly to interpreting the meaning of your daydreams, your shamanic journeys, as well as of your life experiences.

Imagine, everyone in your life is another you, an external aspect, and a reflection of you that you can learn from. The Mayans understand this to be true, as reflected in their saying, "In lak'ech," meaning 'you are another me.'

The Shamanic Body Map

One of my favorite mapping systems is that of the Shamanic Body Map. This symbol system is a direct teaching of 'As above, so below,' as this symbol system is a map of consciousness. What exists in the physical is a direct reflection of what is held in the mental and emotional levels. The body is a mirror of the inner, unseen world of both personality and soul.

The body is highly symbolic. The body will reflect that emotional and mental upset through various symptoms, illness, and dis-ease. If you are happy and joyful, your body will reveal that state of well-being.

Treating the physical body alone for illness is a limited and finite approach. Yet, when you can understand what the body is telling you about its lack of harmony, you can treat the causal energies of spiritual, emotional, and mental discord. In this manner, you may return to balance and restore your physical health. This is the foundation of shamanic healing, to treat the spiritual cause of disharmony.

Other Symbol Systems to Explore

These are but a few of the symbol systems, or shamanic map systems, to assist you in greater mastery of your soul's journey and earth walk. They are an excellent foundation for finding your soul's map and directional guidance system as you do your best to live a harmonious life. Other symbol systems you may want to explore include but are not limited to astrology, numerology, divination systems (tarot, oracles, runes, etc.), family constellation work, and cards of destiny.

White Dog
Katherine Skaggs © 2017

SECTION 2

AWAKENING YOUR ARTIST, SHAMAN, HEALER, SAGE

WITHIN YOUR VERY BEING RESIDES AN AWAKENED BEING: THE ARTIST, SHAMAN, HEALER, AND SAGE

The Artist, the Shaman, the Healer, and the Sage are powerful archetypal energies that live inside of you. As you embody each one, they will empower you to create your life consciously and powerfully.

When you connect to the Artist within, you awaken the powers of your creative nature, your imagination, your curiosity, and wonderment.

As you align with your inner Shaman, your illuminated heart awakens, giving you the freedom of soul flight and the ability to see from the perspective of Spirit. Connecting to your inner Healer activates the healing powers of alchemy, magic, and transformation. The inner Healer gives you the power to shapeshift your reality from mundane to magical.

As you honor yourself and all of your experiences as sacred on the adventure of the earth walk, you activate your inner Sage. The inner Sage is the wise one and keeper of the wisdom that comes through experience and inner reflection.

Getting to know your own unique, inner Artist, Shaman, Healer, and Sage can be valuable, if not crucial, in how you experience your earth walk with power and grace. Within the individual chapters devoted to the Artist, the Shaman, the Healer, and the Sage, you will find in-depth shamanic teachings, practices, and specific shamanic medicines associated with these archetypes that will assist you in the exploration of these powers within your own self.

Get to know each archetype, their medicine, and their powers, so you are familiar with each one. Do your best to embody each quality through inner reflection, imagination, and action through the practices given.

Empowerment comes when you begin to express each archetype with purpose and intention. As you connect to the energy and essence of each archetype, you will begin to experience a greater sense of wholeness, being more authentically yourself, empowered, creative, and awake within the dream of life.

Bendiciones de la Familia
Katherine Skaggs © 2010

*T*he *Bendiciones de la Familia* painting was created as a *prayerful blessing from a vision I received as I hiked down the sacred Huichol mountain of Cerro Quemado near the town of Real de Catorce, Mexico. I had been in ceremony since early morning, deep in prayer upon this mountain hike. As I came back* *down the mountain I was reflecting upon specific prayers I had for a dear young woman friend and her husband who were trying to get pregnant. As I reflected, Virgin de Guadalupe, the Aztec Great Mother of these lands, and Grandfather (who is a mix of a Huichol shaman Guadalupe, Grandfather Peyote, and Jesus) came to me. They showed me a successful pregnancy and birth, bringing this sacred child to this couple, held within their protection and blessings. Blue Deer's presence on the horizon not only insured the safe birth of this child, but also the promise of a second child to come at a future time. With the sun in the upper right hand corner, and Peyote on the right lower part of the painting, and vast amounts of roses on the left, great protection and blessings surrounded this family and their happy life to unfold. (All has since come to pass since this painted prayer blessing. The first child was even born underneath the painting!)*

Dream a New Dream
Katherine Skaggs © 2009

CHAPTER 3

THE ARTIST SHAMAN
HEALER SAGE

WITHIN YOUR VERY BEING RESIDES THE CREATIVE SPARK OF THE ARTIST

Imagination, Curiosity, and Childlike Wonderment
Creation & Sacred Destruction - Freedom
Animal Totem Spider
Plant Spirit Medicine Albacha
Stone Spirit Medicine Clear Quartz
Ritual Art Making

Naturally, each of us is a creative being, born of Great Spirit, the Divine Creative Giver of Life. Shamanic tribes and cultures worldwide are artisans in every expression: dancers, storytellers, painters, magicians, shapeshifters, pattern makers, singers, shamanic tool makers, carvers, craftsman, and healers — the shamans, the medicine men, and women. Their creativity connects them to the essence of Creation, bringing harmony and beauty wherever they are. At the core of every great shaman healer is the Artist who can shift a tangled energy pattern by artfully creating a harmonious design to restore balance.

*E*very child is an artist; the problem is staying an artist when you grow up.

~ Pablo Picasso

Outside shamanic cultures, most of us are living in the culture of the left brain. This reasoning-based world too often devalues the creativity that lives within. This world has lost its magic, as it is linear, tethered from one moment to the next, defined by achievement, money, and outward appearances.

Even if you weren't born in a shamanic culture, creativity — your ability to create and reshape your dream — is your Divine heritage. It lives in every aspect of your DNA. Your creative, artisan self now calls to you to activate your superpowers of imagination, to reconnect to your soul's creative powers, and to dream your world anew.

What if infinite realities are awaiting you and your heart's desires? Are you ready?

The Creative Spark
You Are the Dreamer of Your Reality

Imagination, curiosity, and childlike wonderment are your superpowers! The Creative Spark, your Artist shaman self, works magically within the portal of your imagination to embrace the possibility and potential of creation in every aspect of your life.

Imagination, curiosity, and childlike wonderment are your soul's superpowers.

Can you remember being a child and playing 'pretend?' What did you daydream about? Who did you want to be when you grew up? Now, as an adult, what do you imagine? What are you curious about?

Do You Still Possess Childlike Wonderment?

When you engage your imagination with clear intention, focus, and heart-centeredness, you discover the power to create any reality. The act of being curious like a child gives access to the power of the quantum field and the Great Void, also known as the Cosmic Womb. Unlimited, creative answers and energy come into your awareness, aligning with your focus to create the life you desire.

What do you really want? Where does your passion lie? What have you always wanted to do or to create?

Whether small or big, when you focus on your true heart's desires to create any one thing, you activate the powers of Creation through your inner Artist self. Now is when the Universe and quantum field begin to assist you and bring your dreams into reality.

Imagine now that YOU are the one who indeed dreams your life each day. The more you are curious about something you haven't experienced, when combined with your heart's desire, you begin to draw that imagining to you. When you start to wonder, "What if…? or What would it be like if…?" you begin to stir the quantum field of possibility. By doing so, by wondering, the quantum field MUST answer you. In the vocabulary of shamanism, Great Spirit, your spirit allies, guides, angels, and spirit animals, MUST also answer you. The more excited you get, the more focused you get, the more you express in the innocence of a child's wonderment, the more clearly you create what your heart's desires. All of Creation MUST answer your curious imaginings.

Be aware too that if you are wondering how bad it can get, the Universe will answer in like kind. It is most important to focus on what truly pleases you. Suppose you are struggling to find your curious, childlike wonderment and imagination for what is positive. In that case, it is time to clean your thoughts and your energy through shamanic practices, such as grounding, smudging, connecting to nature, and prayer. Shift your perspective upward so as NOT to create through fear.

Are you creating intentionally and working in harmony with the world around you? Do you act upon your imaginings and visions? The expression of that imagination depends on how you focus your energy and attention. Are you creating from the innocence of a child or the wounds born of rough times? Are you conscious of your focus and energy? Or are you unconsciously creating and 'spinning' tangled webs?

Pele, Hawaiian Goddess of Volcanoes
Katherine Skaggs © 2009

Divine Mama Pele brings the fire of purification to clean away disrespect and desecration of unconscious thoughts and actions, to return balance and bring new life. Pele is the Mother of Fire, being the primal force that brings transformation that leads to healing and reintegration into wholeness.

The Artist Works with the Powers of Both Creation and Sacred Destruction

I find it is essential to understand that every time you create, that you also let go of what was. Each time an artist puts paint on a canvas, she lets go of the blank canvas. It is gone, over and done. It is a core shamanic truth that each time you create something new, an old way and form dies. And conversely, when you release an old way of being, an old pattern and old identity, new life begins.

This is the power of sacred destruction, death, and release that also comes through creative acts. The Artist shaman self creates with intention and clarity of mind and heart. She consciously uses ceremony and ritual to give birth to her ideas in a sacred manner. And she honors the death of her old ways of being with gratitude, celebration, and ruthless releasing rituals.

> You cannot move forward into a new life if you hold onto an old story of the past.

If you want to create change within yourself and your life, you cannot hold on to the past. This includes forgiving all hurtful or traumatic experiences that have defined you. Conversely, if you want to grow, you also must release the old identities born of your accomplishments, glory moments, and degrees that have defined you. To be free, all of these stories must also die. You are not your story. Life evolves, and so do you.

The Artist self embodies the truth that 'You are the Dreamer of your reality." You are the writer and director of your story and your life experience. You choose every character in the play of life, whether it is a beautiful musical, a comedy, or a horror story. You have the power as the Artist, the editor, the director, and the decision-maker of this life! If you don't like one of the chapters in your book of life, you have the authority and power to change it. With this comes freedom.

The Artist's Sacred Destruction Ritual
and Ceremony To Bless, to Release, and to Create Anew

If there is any place in the past that has held you captive, it is time for change. It is time to begin imagining anew, wondering what blessings are in store for you as you release the old, past stories. What if you are ready for a rebirth that is far better than anything you have ever imagined or experienced now?

It is crucial to release the bonds of the past so you can grow. Here's a great ritual for letting go of the old, so you can imagine and create a new way of life.

~ Block out time for yourself and your ceremony. It might be an hour or a day.

~ Create a sacred space for yourself away from others, electronic devices, and distractions. Great places might include your meditation room, in front of your altar, at a fire pit or fireplace, or a place in nature where you can be still and quiet. This can be any place where you are safe, quiet, and can be inwardly focused.

~ Gather Items for your Sacred Destruction Ritual and Ceremony:

~ Sage, palo santo, sacred tobacco, or incense that pleases.

- A lighter.

- Paper - A large piece for drawing or painting on.

- Colored pens, markers, pencils, or paints.

- Kindling and wood for fire pit (charcoal or small wood for an indoor container.)

- Fire pit, cauldron, or safe container for burning the paper.

~ Light the sage, palo santo, or sacred incense to set a clean and sacred space.

- Let the smoke bathe your physical body and energy.

- Smoke the location you are in.

- Smoke the materials you have gathered for your sacred ceremony and ritual.

- Call upon your spirit guides and helpers, especially the Masters of Creation and Sacred Destruction.

- Call upon the experts of owl and snake to assist you.

- Acknowledge your spirit allies (even if you have no idea who they are). Say something like, "Thank you for your powers. Thank you for being here to assist me now. Thank you for keeping me safe and for releasing me from the past patterns that limit my joy."

- Or create your own expression of gratitude to your helpers and acknowledge their expertise in supporting you now.

~ Reflect upon an experience or chapter of your life that you are ready to let go of, that you believe has defined and limited you, for better or worse, and prepare for transformation.

~ Call forth the courage and willingness to completely surrender the old, past stories.

~ What experiences have held you captive, blocked your creativity, and dampened your spirit? Identify the limiting thoughts, feelings, stories, and beliefs that get in the way of you creating the life you desire.

~ Sit in reflection and notice what arises in your mind, your emotions, and your body. Are you angry? Depressed? Numb? Sick? In lack? In greed and envy? Is there a story of "I can't because…" or "_____ did this to me."

~ Write the story and qualities of the old identity and experience you want to release (the good, the bad, the ugly) onto a sheet(s) of paper. Write in detail as much as you desire. The juicier, the better. Include how you feel, what you like and don't like, as well as any fear-based, limiting beliefs that need to leave in the process. This is a time to truly let go, as well as to make sacred what you have experienced, whether joyful or terrible.

~ Once the thoughts, emotions, and energies arise into your awareness, grab a color (pen/paint/pencil) and do your best to express this onto the paper. Express your feelings by expressively making your mark, painting the color, or writing the words on the paper. I cannot encourage you enough to let the emotion flow through your body and not just your mind. Make your mark! Ask your body to fully express this through the action of making your mark. Ask your mind to let go. Ask your emotions to let go. Do this as a sacred act of love as you let go of what is not in harmony. Let it all go.

~ Give yourself as much time as you desire. Trust your intuition and imagination as you release these old patterns, vibrations, emotions, thoughts, and stories onto paper. Be in conversation with them. THANK them for all they have taught you. Bless them. Release any judgment as this energy moves out of you. Invite the Spirit of Trust to guide you into a new life with the wisdom born of this 'death.'

- Once you have released everything onto paper, sit, breathe, and be present to yourself. Honor your courage for releasing this energy and the stories of the past.
- As you let go of the old story, through your intention, claim the Artist shaman's power to create a new life and new experience.
- In gratitude, light the smudge and bless yourself with its smoke, cleaning any residual negative energy. Smudge the paper and your story for additional cleansing and blessing.
- Speak words of love and kindness, compassion to yourself. You are now a newborn, cleaned of the old, ready for new experiences. Acknowledge your transformation.
- Now, light the fire in your cauldron, fire pit, fireplace, or fire-safe container (even a large cooking pot with a lid.) Thank the Spirit of Fire for its equal powers of sacred destruction and of transformation.
- Take your paper and bless it and all that it represents by speaking any words of gratitude and blessing. You might say something like speaking loudly to Great Spirit: "Thank you for all you have taught me through these experiences. I am now complete and release all patterns of fear, trauma, and old ways of being that no longer serve my highest good. I release through all time, space, dimensions, alternate realities, and time-space continuums. I receive all the teachings, wisdom, and blessings that come from these experiences."
- Now, tear the paper up into as many pieces as you desire, further dismantling the past patterns.
- Consciously release these past stories into the fire, in silence or out loud in prayer. Notice how the fire burns even more brightly each time you release the old into it, giving more energy and life to you now!
- Acknowledge what is being born anew through the death and release of the old.
- When you have released all the paper and patterns into the fire, speak confidently out loud, "It is done."
- Stand in the energy of the fire, soaking in its warmth and high-frequency energies of Sami that radiate through your

energy field. Take it in. Receive it. This is the energy of your new life.

~ Sit with the fire as it burns down, as part of your ritual, burning away all that you have released and filling with Sami.

~ It is now time for a rest. Go within. Get a good sleep.

Once you experience the Artisan's powers of sacred destruction, it is natural to go within to rest, integrate, and regenerate. Once rested, you are ready and able to begin anew, creating your heart's desires.

Animal Totem Spider and Her Medicine

The Artist self can call upon many totems and spirit helpers, as needed, for their expertise. Yet Spider medicine is a perfect animal totem for supporting your Artist archetype with its remarkable ability to awaken the power of creativity. Call upon Spider to assist you in weaving the web of your life.

Spider Medicine assists the Artist in birth and death, creation and destruction. Spider is the Grandmother Weaver of Life, using sound as the real creative force of the Universe. She will tell you to pay attention to your words and communications and to express them with clear intention and the power of love. For these sound vibrations, give life to that which you only imagined. Your words are the creative magic that manifests life. Your intention, plus emotion, create a sound vibration through each syllable, and each word, weaving an invisible song web. This song web expresses and attracts energy, manifesting form, and experience. Grandmother Spider reminds you that your words have energy and have the power to create. Be mindful.

The Shadow Medicine of Spider warns you to take stock in your creative process. Are you truly following your heart and creating what fulfills you?

In Hinduism's shamanic teachings, Spider also brings the powerful medicine of death, as it watches its prey become entangled in her web. What if the prey represents the ego's fear and all patterns of separation from Spirit? If, for any reason, you have unconsciously woven a web of entanglement, call upon Spider and the power of death to release the Hucha, so you may weave your life in harmony.

Sit still now and ask Grandmother Spider to help you. Ask for her support as you honestly evaluate the patterns you have woven into your life. What are your real heart's desires? Are you living in the creative flow and weaving magic into your life through your own creative intentions, words, and actions? Do you give love to each desire, or do you speak and act out of distorted patterns of illusion and fear, critical of yourself and the world around you? If you feel criticism, anger, jealousy, envy, and desire to be like another, you have fallen into the trap of separation. You are entangled in a web of illusion that is of your own making.

Other shadow patterns to look at: Do you create what you 'think' you have to rather than what you desire? (Such as a dead-end job, unfulfilling relationship, etc.?) Have you become a workaholic, self-absorbed, or over-involved in some part of your life, falling out of balance? Have you become distracted through the envy of other's talents or accomplishments, rather than focusing on your own creativity? Do you need to write, draw, or to engage yourself in some act of creativity? Have you procrastinated acting on something meaningful in your life? Is it time to finish a creative project or move on to a desire in your life?

As with any ally, to receive Spider's assistance, offer her gratitude, love, blessings, and any offerings you like. This is the shamanic path of reciprocity, which is the power that makes the world go around. You and Spider will increase the depth of your ally relationship through reciprocity. She is filled with energy and light by your blessings and is ready to give again.

Plant Spirit Medicine of Tulsi (Holy Basil), aka Rainforest Spirit of Albacha

The Artist shaman self has many signature plant spirit helpers who also help her create her life with power. Yet, we'll begin with the plant spirit known as Albacha to the shamans in the Amazonian jungles of Peru. She is known to spiritual seekers in India by the names of Tulsi or Holy Basil. Albacha is the perfect ally for awakening the profound, inner visionary aspects of the Artist shaman self within.

Albacha is a slightly different strain of Holy Basil than what you will find in India, yet it is none the less potent. Peruvian shamans know this plant medicine to be a powerful purifier of mind, body, and spirit. Albacha increases mental clarity, balances energy, and opens spiritual channels so you may receive higher Divine guidance and vision. Albacha promotes relaxation physically and spiritually, thus integrating your visions, dreams, and spiritual guidance into your life's experiences.

Use Albacha in plant baths and direct application to the body to bring spiritual protection and relaxation. Steep leaves into a tea to increase your ability to go more deeply into meditative, visionary, dream states. This plant spirit supports the Artist's playful nature and ability to create freely from the place of clarity, insight, and harmony within and without.

The Stone Spirit Medicine of Clear Quartz

Clear quartz is a great medicine stone for anyone, any time, and should be a part of any medicine bag, altar, and ritual space. These crystals are excellent conductors, intensifying your intentions, hopes, and dreams, as well as the energy of other stones. Clear quartz is perfect for the creative Artist shaman to use as a generator and amplifier of her visions and creative desires.

It will store your prayers and intentions and give them energy for expansion. It is a foundational stone to add to your medicine bag. It is also excellent to wear as an amulet or necklace; put within an energy grid; carry in your pocket; or use as a magic wand for manifestation.

~ Work with clear quartz when you are visioning and planting seeds for new creations in your life.

~ Smudge the stone before speaking your prayers into it, focusing on clearing old programming, so it is ready for your new intentions.

~ Sing, speak and pray into the stone in gratitude for sending your prayers to Spirit.

~ Then sit with it in prayer and silence and connect your heart to the essence of the stone. Be open to any communication in return as you sit with the power and presence of this stone being helper.

~ When you feel complete, place the stone on the altar in the position of the East, the direction of new beginnings.

Shamanic Ritual Art Making

Many shamanic practices are perfect for awakening the spirit of the Artist shaman self. All creative endeavors, coupled with prayer, ritual, and ceremony, are excellent practices. These include but are not limited to singing, chanting, drumming, trance dancing, shamanic tool making, and ritual art-making.

Shamanic Ritual Art Making is precisely that; uniting prayer, intention, ritual, and ceremony into the creative expression we call art. Any intentional creative expression we call art gives birth to an expansive spiritual expression and awareness. This can be painting, drawing, sculpting, beading, felting, sacred doll making, trance dance, chanting, shamanic song, and music-making of any sort. The practice of holy ritual art-making is one that bleeds into every aspect of intentionally creating your life. It also is an excellent way to move into altered states of awareness through your creativity.

When I make a shamanic tool or teach others to make shamanic tools, it is always within ritual and ceremony.

What would you like to create? What are the creative materials you would like to use?

Make Your Own Shamanic Medicine Wand!

Let's begin by making a shamanic medicine wand. This is an excellent shamanic tool and art-making process that gets you working with nature, your intuition, and the inner Artist self. It is an embodiment of not only your creativity but your magic. Once created, your wand is an excellent tool to direct your focus to your goals, clear energy, invoke allies, and manifest your dreams.

~ Take a nature walk and open to the medicine of Spirit through the natural world. As you take your walk, set an intention that you will find one or more unique sticks suitable for adding feathers, stones, and sacred items to.

~ Now, say a prayer to call the spirit of this stick to you on your walk. "Hello, Stick spirit, where are you? Please come to me with your medicine and assist me in bringing forth magic and medicine for my life."

~ Upon embarking on your walk, still your mind, with a clear intention that at least one stick spirit will call to you. You will know or feel that you must pick up a particular stick. When this happens, know that this stick is the one! Do the same as you look for feathers and other natural objects that may make up your medicine wand.

~ What sticks call to you that are on your path? Are there stone beings saying, "Come here, pick me up"? Have feathers fallen onto your path, waiting for you to retrieve them? Go into the realm of nature to find the medicine that Spirit wants to give you today.

  ▪ Gather sticks, stones, feathers, trinkets, leather, beads, and whatever ignites magic and creativity for your wand. Look for items on nature walks, ventures to your favorite metaphysical stores, 'mountain man' retreats, or wherever you are called. Imagine your Medicine Wand is also a magic wand to help you create the life you want to experience!

~ Set a place to play and create. Consecrate your creative space with smudge (sage, palo santo, or incense) to make it a sacred ritual space.

~ Now, smoke all your items with your favorite smudge.

~ Still yourself into prayer. With gratitude, call forth spirit helpers to assist you in your creative process.

~ If you desire, play drumming, flute, or other shamanic music to further focus you on your creative tool making.

~ Center yourself into the creative process, losing your critical, reasoning mind. Open to the guidance and inner voice of your Artist shaman self!

~ Unite with the spirit of the stick and each item that wants to be part of your medicine wand.

~ Now, create!

~ When you feel complete, bless your medicine wand and sacred art creation for its power and medicine. Notice your prayers and connection.

~ Offer smoke, essential oils, and most of all, your awareness and energy exchange.

~ Ask the spirit of your medicine wand to teach you about further connection and how to command the energy of creation. It will show you what you need to know.

White Eagle
Katherine Skaggs © 2013

CHAPTER 4

THE ARTIST SHAMAN
HEALER SAGE

WITHIN YOUR VERY BEING LIVES THE KNOWER AND THE ILLUMINATED ONE

- Shamanic Medicine of the Illuminated Heart - the Christ, the Buddha, and the Mystic
- The Seer and the Power of Sight
- Animal Totem Eagle
- Plant Spirit Medicine Blue Lotus
- Stone Spirit Medicine Moonstone
- Shamanic Journey with Eagle

The awakened Shaman self is the Knower who lives in our heart, the one who sees from the 'eyes' of our heart. This vital soul aspect is illuminated, wise, humble, empowered, awake, aware, and Christ-like. She can see through the illusions of the physical, ordinary reality world, always knowing the truth of Spirit and the love of Spirit.

Whether you have become aware of it or not, within your very being lives the Shaman, the mystic, the Christ, the Buddha! This is the part of you who is awake, aware of your multi-dimensionality, who knows of your soul's existence in human and other dimensions.

She is the one who flies free of human constraints and is full of vision. The inner Shaman can see, sense, feel, and know the workings of Spirit in all things. Your inner Shaman self creates and directs your reality from the soul's perspective. The inner Shaman implicitly trusts and follows her heart, as she knows it is her spiritual GPS guidance system.

The Shaman self completely understands and knows that she is connected to Spirit and that all is well, no matter the appearance of things in the earthly world. There is always deep trust, knowing the cycles of life have purpose and meaning, and that the earth walk is a grand adventure of the soul. The inner Shaman self knows the deeper spiritual meaning of life, regardless of the outer workings of the world. She understands the blueprint for the soul's growth and for the growth of the whole of humanity. The inner Shaman self absolutely knows and trusts that 'All is well, no matter the appearances of things.'

Shamanic Medicine of the Illuminated Heart - The Christ, the Buddha, and the Mystic

Love is the only answer
No matter the question or situation.

Cultivating your knowing inner Shaman self is a tempered path born of cultivating light, wisdom, truth, love, and compassion. The path of the enlightened Shaman is also that of the Buddha, the Christ, the Bodhisattva.

Initiation, Shamanic Death and Dismemberment

Doesn't it Sound Wonderful to be the Christed One,
the Awakened Shaman, the Buddha?

This is an awe-inspiring endeavor for any soul, as it is a very challenging path that requires sacrifice, initiation, tempering, and death of the smaller-self ego. There will be times of facing anguish, loss, injustice, death of a loved one, ill health that nearly kills you, financial ruin, and many other challenges in relinquishing all attachments of the physical world.

Purple Buddha
Katherine Skaggs © 2004

Just as Mother Mary had to release Jesus, you, too, may need to release someone that you are attached to, and to whom you believe you cannot live without. This is not a certainty but a possibility you must allow yourself to be open to, as those persons who need releasing from our lives can otherwise block the doorway to further spiritual growth. At the very least, you may need to release any patterns the relationship is expressing that are out of harmony and out of balance. Be open to a complete transformation of the relationship.

Face any fear that is expressing in the relationship, within yourself or the other. Then, commit to cleaning this within your own self. This will move you to greater love and harmony within yourself, as well as with another. Then you will be free!

This initiatory path will bring you to deep understandings of the infinite, benevolent, loving eternal essence of Spirit, within and all around, no matter the challenges and appearances of things experienced on the human journey. They are designed to focus you inward, so you more easily listen and follow your heart's guidance. The wisdom of the Divine speaks through your heart space. The external linear world will no longer limit you and your future as you trust your inner voice. For on this path, there is a 'death and dismemberment,' a taking apart of the ego and lower human personality so that you may transcend into a higher state of consciousness, known as the Awakened One, born of the inner Shaman self.

This initiatory path requires a deep, unwavering commitment to Spirit and the Divine. Through this unwavering commitment and focus, you will come to know that the way of Truth is the way of Love, for Divine Love is always the only answer, no matter the question.

A most important part of cultivating the inner Shaman Self soul awareness is to cultivate the wholehearted self. Pay attention to your heart space. Do you lead with your heart, or do you lead with your mind?

Shamanic Journey to Stalk the Ego, and to Awaken the Inner Shaman

To awaken the whole heart and the inner Shaman, find practices that help clean away judgment, trauma, and fear. Look at all the ways your lower ego-based personality wants to control its destiny.

To stalk your lower ego, admit and then take responsibility for hidden or known limiting beliefs, attitudes, and experiences of wounding that distort your reality and move you to choose through fear. You will heal through practices of compassion and forgiveness.

Once we can relax and let go of fear and trauma, our hearts soften. We return home to the soul's power of an open heart. Cultivating unconditional love and compassion are the restorative medicines needed to heal these wounded soul parts.

~ Set your space to create ritual and ceremony by smudging and clearing the space.

~ Put a journal and pen or pencil near you for writing. Write down the date and intention for your shamanic journey. Then return at the end of the journey to record your experience.

~ Turn off all your digital devices and let your family know that you are to be left undisturbed for the entirety of your time within.

~ Lie down within a darkened room, or with an eye mask on to help you move within.

~ Set your intention to awaken your whole heart and inner Shaman self as you release any blocks or limitations of the smaller ego-self.

~ Call in a guide or spirit helper to assist you in your process. Notice who arrives to support you. You can communicate with them through the entire journey for assistance and support.

~ Play a 15- to 30-minute shamanic drum track or trance dance music to move you inwards to altered states.

~ Focus on your heart's intention as you move within.

~ Sit or lie in stillness. Close your eyes.

~ Breathe in deeply, to the count of four, hold for the count of four, out to the count of four, holding your breath again to a count of four. Repeat until you are deeply relaxed.

~ Allow the beat of the drum music to help you lose your linear mind as you go within and to open to your imagination and subconscious. Open to imagery, knowing, feeling, imagination, your inner voice, and all ways you perceive intuitive knowing.

~ If any limiting thoughts, beliefs, or feelings arise, imagine them pouring out of you and your body into Mother Earth, where she eats these energies, freeing you from limitation. Then refocus on your breath and your intention.

~ What stories and symbolism arise?

~ When the music ends, breathe your awareness and your essence back to your body, breathing in from crown to toe. Tell yourself to come all the way home, to your body, now.

~ Once you are fully back to your body and grounded, record your experience in your journal, regarding the guides who showed up, the depth of the experience, with the feelings and thoughts. Write all your symbols down within the experience, then look up their meaning and essence if you need to learn more about them.

~ Note any revelations and wisdom that may have come.

The Seer and the Power of Sight

The actual definition of the word 'shaman' comes from the Manchu-Tungus word šaman, meaning one who knows or one who sees. Some interpret it as "one who sees through the dark." Imagine, as you awaken this aspect within your own archetypal system, that you move into greater spiritual sight, able to 'see' clearly beyond the illusion of the physical, ordinary reality world. This is the sight of the Seer, and the one in the tribe who knows where to hunt, who knows the weather before it arrives, and who can see the patterns that create reality. In modern times the Seer is the one who follows the soul path of the heart. She easily moves beyond the illusions and distractions of duality. This is the one who is connected to the heart of Great Spirit and can truly 'see' through shamanic 'eyes' the Spirit within all life, untainted by ego.

To awaken your inner Shaman's sight requires the practices of meditation, reflection, purification, shamanic journey, and vision quest, to name a few. You must also cleanse your heart of fear, so the eyes of your heart may awaken, not just your third eye. The true sight can only come through a pure heart.

Animal Totem Eagle and Her Medicine

Eagle Medicine brings the powers of the visionary Shaman self, united with the Divine sight of Great Spirit. Eagle flies high to bring the perspective of Great Spirit, yet with a keenness to see even the smallest details on the earth. Eagle lives in the world of Spirit yet can stay grounded in the earth world, balanced between Heaven and Earth. This higher perspective assists you create your earthly life with vision and wisdom messages from Spirit. Call upon Eagle to receive these medicines and the additional blessings of intuition, creativity, strength, courage, hope, healing, and resilience.

Many shamanic cultures also see Eagle commanding both sun and thunder elements, bringing the energy of illumination and sudden knowing. The Aztecs, Sumerians, Egyptians, and Native American tribes also find freedom in Eagle's medicine.

Eagle Totem
Katherine Skaggs © 2010

As a predator, Eagle brings the wisdom of balance to the Artist, the Shaman, the Healer, and the Sage self. To do so, Eagle consumes the weak and sick aspects of creation, preventing the spread of disease. It is a valuable practice to give Eagle any and all 'sick' aspects of your life that are not viable or vital. This is again the perfect union of the Artist, Shaman, Healer, Sage, cleaning and transforming the soul and the human experience.

As you awaken your inner Shaman, you will find Eagle to be the perfect ally for giving you Spirit's sight to dream your world into harmony through alignment with higher principles, wisdom, and vibrations.

The Shadow Medicine of Eagle appears when you are unable to envision a new life and have fallen to Earth in the shadow of Eagle. You are mired in a single perspective, unable to lift above the din of ordinary reality. Most likely, you feel spiritually lost, without guidance, without vision and direction, and possibly all alone. You may literally find yourself looking down all the time, feeling down, depressed, and unable to hope. You may experience the wound of abandonment and betrayal. You are weak, have lost your creativity, and possibly your connection to Spirit. You are unable to fly freely in your life as you desire.

If the shadows have clipped your wings to fly high, it is time to call upon Eagle to lift your spirit and to give you the healing medicines of the Divine.

> Eagle says, "Open your mind now. Open your heart now. Open! Sit erect and lift your head. Look up. Sit up! Connect upwards."

Hike to the top of a hill or mountain, look across the horizon, or visualize the same. Move your focus to a physically higher focal point. Change your point of view. Both the physical and spiritual will align to a higher place when you do so.

Step out of your habits, loosen your wings, loosen your mental thoughts, and loosen your heart center. Pull your shoulders back, feeling your shoulder blades come toward one another, opening your chest and heart space, opening to your courage and hope, and activating the wings of your spiritual being to take flight.

But for you to take flight, your heart must once again open. You must discard your mental constrictions and awaken your sacred heart, for Great Spirit and Eagle live within the portal of your sacred heart, awaiting your attention.

Eagle says if you want to open your heart and access the power of Eagle and Great Spirit, you must release judgment and criticism, especially of yourself. Extend unconditional acceptance to any parts of yourself that have fallen victim to criticism, judgment, and separation from your true nature of love. Extend compassion and kindness to yourself.

Plant Spirit Medicine of Blue Lotus

Blue Lotus is an ancient, psychoactive plant medicine used in Egyptian, Hindu, Mayan, Syrian, and Thai rituals and ceremonies to bring visions and to awaken intuition and deep spiritual knowing. This plant medicine is a shamanic sacrament that brings tranquility and is known to increase the dream state.

Lotus itself is a symbol of the soul's journey to awakening, rising out of the mud to blossom clean and beautiful, symbolizing purity, illumination, and resurrection. In Buddhism, the blue lotus symbolizes victory over the senses, representing intelligence, wisdom, and knowledge.

This is the perfect plant medicine to assist you in awakening your inner Shaman self. The priests and priestess of ancient Egypt drank blue lotus tea to enter into a dreamy, altered state. This enabled them to 'see' more clearly from the realm of Spirit, free of ego and attachment.

Drink blue lotus tea in sacred ceremonial spaces to go deep within shamanic journey spaces, calming and relaxing the physical self, allowing the soul to fly free into heightened states of awareness.

The Stone Spirit Medicine of Moonstone

Moonstone works perfectly to support and illuminate the Shaman self. It assists in accessing the deep, lush, inner reflective spaces of your soul. This pearlescent stone helps us tap into our intuitive, psychic, clairvoyant, knowing nature. This stone offers the Divine Feminine energies of creativity, intuition, and inspiration.

Moonstone also empowers the inner Shaman self with the powers of introspection, strength, and discernment. Moonstone can assist us in smoothing emotional instability and stress, bringing calm and centeredness.

Wear Moonstone near your heart to open your heart space, balance your emotions, and to activate the power of your soul's true desires. To increase dreams and visions, place it under your bed or under your pillow at night. Hold in your hands or place on your crown or third eye when meditating and asking for inspiration. Use in shamanic journey spaces to access the depths of your soul's power to fly into the inner realms of Spirit. This is another excellent stone to have in your medicine bag or bundle. Place with intention and prayer on your altar.

Take a Shamanic Journey with Eagle to Awaken Your Heart and Activate Your Ability to Fly

Focus your intentions for opening your heart as you begin your shamanic journey to gain vision and clarity on your earth walk, as well as to awaken in the dream.

~ Create a safe space to lie down and go within, whether in a bedroom, meditation room, or altar space.

~ Smudge the room with sage or your favorite smudge herb.

~ Say 'hello' to your spirit allies and helpers and ask them to hold a protective space of nothing but light and love.

~ Then ask your spirit helper Eagle to take you on a journey within, to awaken your heart space, and to illuminate the eyes of your soul, giving you sight and clarity.

~ Play some repetitive shamanic journey drum music or shamanic trance meditation music to support your journey within.

~ Focus clearly on your intentions to connect with Eagle and the healing medicine you need now. In your imagination, open a portal in a cloud or somewhere in the sky, where you can hop onto Eagle's back and fly high into the heavenly realm.

~ You might even become Eagle as you feel the air under your wings and lift away from the limited perspective you have had.

~ Feel the freedom of flight and notice how it feels to be above the dense energies of the earthly life and its limited view.

~ What do you notice that is different? How does it feel in your body? Can you feel the love of Great Spirit? Fly high as long as you desire, gathering energy and light, greater sight, and wisdom from this higher point of view.

~ Ask Eagle and Great Spirit to fill your heart with heavenly light.

~ Feel the medicine of Eagle and its feathers and the purifying energies of light cleansing your heart, your body, and your mind.

~ Breathe these light energies into every cell, every organ, every thought, and every emotion.

~ Soak in the blessings of Eagle and Great Spirit, anchoring in light from above to you as the receiving vessel.

~ As you deepen your breath, relax and breathe, be present.

~ Focus a grounding cord down from the root of your spine into Mother Earth, bringing this energy completely to this moment, in your body, into present time.

~ Be aware of what it feels like to be in this energy and sacred space. Notice the different energy and vibrations of your body now, of your feelings, and your thoughts. Calmness, centeredness, full-heartedness, and clarity are common experiences.

~ Return to your body through your intention and your breath, running this energy from crown to toe, through your blood, your bones, your organs, and all your body's systems. Imagine it flowing through your physical, emotional, mental, and spiritual bodies.

~ As you return restored and regenerated, thank Eagle and Great Spirit for opening you to these medicines of heart and sight, and all that came into your experience and awareness. Rest and integrate.

~ Take a moment to reflect upon your journey. Journal important experiences and awareness that came to you.

This is an important practice to support you in deepening your personal revelation through shamanic journey work.

Owl Shaman Jaguar Medicine Healing
Katherine Skaggs © 2011

Chapter 5

THE ARTIST SHAMAN **HEALER** SAGE

Within Your Very Being, Lives the Healer

Shamanic Medicine of the Hollow Bone

The Magician, the Shapeshifter,
the Power of Alchemy

Animal Totem Snake

Plant Spirit Medicine Sacred Tobacco

Stone Spirit Medicine Turquoise

Water to Clean and to Clear

Your Healer shaman self knows that the true power of healing lives within you; your soul is the only one who can heal itself through alignment with your own higher, inner soul self, also aligned to the wholeness and love of Great Spirit. The Healer knows NO separation between the human body, her life force, and the energy of Spirit. She understands that she is dreaming this life from soul to human self. The Healer is the lucid dreamer who can transform her state of consciousness and experience.

The Healer knows:
'There is no outer shaman,
there is no outer healer, YOU are IT!'

Shamanic Medicine of the Hollow Bone

The Healer shaman self is the hollow bone, the hollow reed, and the portal between Great Spirit and the physical world. The hollow bone is the conduit between Heaven and Earth, between the Divine and the ordinary, transmitting energy from above to below, and below to above through her pure vessel.

Awakening your Healer shaman self is an initiatory path that often takes you through the experience of illness and tragedy, through the shadows of the human mind and small ego. This may happen through your own personal journey with physical illness, through an experience of the illness of a loved one, through loss of a loved one, and/or through your own shamanic death and dismemberment process. You may also go through a mental or emotional breakdown as you break away false beliefs, fear, manipulations, trauma, and external pressures to be something that you are not.

This tempering process brings vast spiritual understanding. It is an initiation that transforms you at the deepest emotional levels. You may now love and accept other souls having their human experience in deep compassion, without judgment.

When working with another who is experiencing illness, the Healer shaman self sees the whole soul devoid of illness. At the same time, she is able to recognize the distorted patterns of disease in the energetic and the physical bodies without judgment. In this pure state, the Healer shaman self becomes the hollow bone, a vessel of light, a womb of healing energy. The other soul may rest in this safe healing energy, for the restoration of both the spiritual and physical experience. This is a high vibrational state that returns the soul to union with Spirit. It is a frequency where miracles and instant transformation can occur.

Even though this sounds like the Healer shaman self is doing all the healing, she is purely a conduit for the light of Spirit to work in union with the desires of the one who is ready to heal.

Become the Hollow Bone Exercise and Meditation

If you truly desire to become the Hollow Bone and to awaken your inner Healer shaman, take time to purify your mind, your body, your heart, and your spirit. Remove doubt and fear while inviting the higher frequencies of love and Great Spirit into your heart.

~ Set a sacred space for yourself by retreating into a quiet spot in your home or in nature. If you have an altar and meditation room or a place of prayer, that is best.

~ Light sage, incense, or your favorite smudge to consecrate your space and your experience as sacred, cleaning the room and your energy field of lower energies.

~ Focus your intentions to receive only light, love, wisdom, and opening to the Divine.

~ Light a candle and say heartfelt prayers to connect your heart to Great Spirit and to the highest frequencies of light and love, that you may be a true Hollow Bone.

~ Call in a spirit guide or totem animal to protect and guide you.

~ Drum or play recorded drumbeats to deepen your inner journey with Spirit.

~ Close your eyes and move your attention into your heart.

~ Imagine there is a beautiful, bright light glowing and expanding in your heart space, as if it is an altar fire to Spirit.

~ Deeply breathe in to the count of seven, connecting your heart light with the in-breath to the eternal flame of Spirit, breathing in love.

~ Hold to the count of four, centering in the eternal flame and love of Spirit.

~ Exhale to the count of seven, releasing all lower energies, fear, doubt, distractions and ego into the flames of Spirit.

~ Repeat this cycle seven to ten times, deepening with each breath in, with each breath out, until you feel deeply relaxed, connected, stilled, and open.

~ From this stillness, invite the light and love of Great Spirit to flow through you, unimpeded by ego or fear, through the light of love.

~ Visualize your physical body, your energy bodies, and your spiritual self, open and luminous. Imagine you are the Hollow Bone. Imagine with all your senses the radiant energy of Great Spirit flowing through you and around you, from heaven to earth.

~ Breathe and surrender to the highest and most Divine energies of Spirit so you may open to the expansive energy, light, love, and wisdom.

~ Sit in your meditation and journey as long as you desire, aligning with this loving flow of energy. Soak it in. Let it overflow through you.

When you feel complete, breathe back to your body, crown to toe, several times until you feel completely grounded and present.

Record your experiences in your journal, taking note of the messages and energy that you experienced. Can you bring this energy into your everyday earth walk?

The more time and focus you take for prayer, breath, shamanic journey, and dream spaces to purify and open to the love, light and energy of Great Spirit, the more you will open your intuitive knowing, and capacity to 'see' the soul clearly in the world of human and ordinary reality. The only way to truly 'see' and 'know' is to have a pure heart, a pure mind, and a pure body. This awakens your ability to be the hollow bone. The human personality of "me, my, mine" clears away from its smallness, allowing the great light of Spirit to shine through you in service to your greater soul self and the greater good of your community.

The Magician and the Shapeshifter

The Healer's Power of Alchemy

The Healer's shamanic medicine of alchemy expresses through the archetypal magic of the inner Magician and the Shapeshifter. The Magician and Shapeshifter Healer align with universal laws and truths, and the invisible world of Spirit to transform and shapeshift one's life miraculously and effortlessly. Miraculously, they create something from seemingly nothing. These magical aspects of the Healer are masterful at taking a life event that perhaps didn't go so well and transforming it to an important and powerful spiritual experience, a miraculous healing, in essence the energetic alchemy of turning lead into gold.

These masters of shamanic alchemy invoke magic and miracles by aligning with the highest frequencies of the Divine, changing the vibrational frequency within a structure or system through the energies of love and wisdom.

Magician and Shapeshifter Totems of Owl and Crow

Owl and crow are two magical, shapeshifting totems of the Magician and Shapeshifter Healer shaman self. Both allies are associated with the Spirit of the West, and wield the powers of death, whereby the ability to dismantle one reality so another may come into form. Their expertise makes them powerful allies of alchemical transformation and magic, with the ability to assist you in shape shifting the circumstances in your life.

Jaguar Shaman Woman
Katherine Skaggs © 2015

Call upon Owl's assistance during rituals where you release old patterns, clear fear, and where you call in your ancestors. If you have had a fearful experience or trauma, owl is one of the best allies to call upon to clear the trauma. Then, you can relax, come back to balance, and move forward with the wisdom gained from your experiences.

Crow is the intelligent, fearless keeper of sacred law and divination, and is associated with everything magical and mystical. Crow brings you the medicine needed to help you align with the magic

Crow Medicine
Katherine Skaggs © 2013

and mystery of Divine Law. Journey with Crow to gain the higher spiritual perspective, of your circumstances. Ask Crow to give you the medicine needed to live in integrity between your heavenly soul self, and your earthly experiences. This will shape shift your circumstances into harmony.

Look for magic when Crow arrives! Pay attention to your heart's knowing regarding your life experiences. Are you in alignment? If not, it is time to go within. Journey to your deepest places of magic and soul desire through meditation, reflection, and shamanic journey. Ask Crow to assist you in accessing your personal magic, and the power of your true soul essence. Align with this magic and the spiritual truth within you through the feeling and vibration of the energies. Ask Crow to show you the actions that will honor your heart and soul desires. Then act, with Crow as your ally, to shapeshift your outer world, even by making the smallest changes. Trust in Crow and the power of Spirit to support you in opening to receive the blessings Great Spirit has for you.

The Magician and Shapeshifter Healer shaman self weaves the soul's matrix into harmonious song patterns through her magic. She often works with plant medicines, stone spirit medicines, light codes, song, sound, movement, art, and spirit allies to invoke healing states.

Shamanic Journey with the West, Owl and Mother Earth to Clear Fear

To cultivate your Healer shaman self, work with the power of the West in the Medicine Wheel as well as the power of Owl as healing allies. The West teaches about the cycles of both harvest and death. It is the cycle of completion, celebration, death, and release. Letting go of old patterns, as well as completing a cycle, are important to healing and transformation. Call in Owl to clean away the vibrations of fear and trauma so light and wisdom may take their place.

The Healer shaman self has mastery in moving through endings, loss, transition, and sudden change. Call to your inner Healer to support you and your world to restore balance as you clear the ego mind and its dark shadows of fear.

~ Create a quiet space to go within.

~ Light some sage, palo santo, or incense to set the container's energy.

~ Turn off all digital devices.

~ Light a candle as you focus on your intentions to connect to the West and to clear any fearful energies that create imbalance.

~ Place a black stone, such as black obsidian or black tourmaline, at the base of your spine, on your root chakra.

~ Place a rose quartz on your heart.

~ Play shamanic drumming or music (15-30 minutes) of your liking that supports you to move into a meditative journey space.

~ Now greet Mother Earth.

~ Imagine dropping a giant root deep from the base of your spine into her center, rooting down into her life force and support.

~ Imagine through your grounding root, that there is a channel that releases hucha into Mother Earth, for her to eat.

~ Honor her for her power to compost, where she is able to 'eat' and transmute what you let go of. Just as she eats carbon dioxide and gives back oxygen, she eats our fear and gives us love.

~ Give her the compost of fear and trauma that may be expressed as judgment (internal or external), greed, envy, lack, hatred, separation, conflict, a lack of peace, illness, an accident, and any experiences, beliefs and attitudes that separate you from joy, love, peace and happiness.

~ As you make your offering to Mother Earth, you may imagine these energies and experiences dropping into the earth, soaking into the ground, or dropping through a hole or portal of some sort.

~ Then, through another channel within your root, imagine soaking in Mother Earth's healing energy and life force. This is her form or reciprocity and gratitude for feeding her your compost.

~ Then, inwardly say 'hello' to both the Spirit of the West and Owl.

~ Thank them for their powerful energies that are here to assist you in letting go of old energy patterns that no longer work, such as any fear patterns, or trauma patterns, whether known or unknown.

~ Honor the West and Owl and their powers, then direct them to go to work to clean you. Direct them to find any and all dense, low frequency energies, and transform them.

~ As the music plays, continue to drift into your imagination, going inward.

~ Call Owl to you now, to eat any fear. You may see, sense, feel, or imagine the Spirit of Owl coming into your body, eating heartache, grief, inability to stomach a situation, etc. Imagine Owl literally taking your body apart to consume any fear and trauma patterns. As you journey with Owl, ask for the lessons and wisdom that come as you let go of these patterns.

~ Now, put your attention on the West. Notice the energy of the West, the sunset and the ending of day, moving into night. Ask the West to draw away any difficult patterns into the sunset, releasing the burdens from your psyche, your emotions, and your physical self.

~ Sit in the dark and the silence. Call all lost soul parts home to you now: joy, innocence, happiness, preciousness, well-being, health, lightness, abundance, creativity, etc.

~ Drop down and feel Mother Earth beneath you, holding you to her.

~ Feel her clearing you and filling you back up with her light and life force.

~ When you are ready, take a deep breath from crown to toe. Do this several times to return to your body, coming all the way home to this present moment, restored and renewed.

~ Relax and rest as you receive the clearing from your allies for as long as you desire.

~ Journal what is most important about your experience when complete.

Animal Totem Snake and Her Medicine

Snake Medicine is similar to that of Spider, as it also brings the powers of birth and death, shedding the skins of illusion and limitation. It is also a symbol of the Serpent Medicine energy of Mother Earth, who, in addition to the powers of birth and death, bring regeneration through her cycles, purifying and transmuting toxins.

Many shamanic cultures, including ancient Goddess cultures, revered Snake as a fertility and Creatrix Goddess. They understood her creative powers that give birth to new life, but also her powers to shed the skins of the old world, transforming everything in the process.

In Hinduism, Snake is the serpent power of the kundalini. Kundalini is your creative, life-giving, healing, and sexual energy. The medicine of the kundalini serpent resides in the base of your spine, coiled 3 1/2 times, awaiting its awakening. When the kundalini serpent begins to awaken, expect everything in your life to change. The fire of Spirit lives within this serpent power. Its ability to transmute fear, trauma, and misunderstandings brings healing on all levels, but most importantly to the soul. The blessings of snake and her kundalini energy bring the power to spiritually awaken, as well as to physically transform and heal.

The Shipibo people in the jungles of Peru will tell you that a giant cosmic anaconda gave birth to the dream of Earth and to all of our existence. In sacred ceremony, the shamans work with their plant medicine ayahuasca which invokes visions of snakes and awakens the kundalini serpent, cleansing the soul, and healing the spirit.

Call upon the medicine of Snake to assist you in shedding the skins of toxins and energies born of the past so you may return to balance and harmony. Journey with Snake, invoking her to use her healing powers to transmute and transform poison in your life.

The Shadow Medicine of Snake brings a warning to wake up, to create intentionally, and to shed the past identities that constrict your growth and experience. Are you in the shadows of Snake's creative and enlightening medicine, afraid, even frozen, and separate from your creative process? If so, it is time to call upon Snake to assist you in transmuting the poisons in your dream of human life, so that you may then shed the fear, wounding, and trauma of the past.

Snake encourages you to surrender all that limits you, to surrender the poison and heavy skins of illusion. If you want to transmute what has poisoned you, you must be willing and committed to the process. If you don't surrender, you won't be able to heal, nor will you be able create anew. You will be stuck in patterns of suffering born of the past, unable to change.

To access the medicine of Snake, work with shamanic journey, visualization, breath work, and meditation. Merge with the medicine of Snake that you may awaken your creative, sensual, healing nature. Connect to this power, breathing it from root to crown, to awaken self-healing and vitality for life. Trust your instincts to know how to move, how to breathe, how to best shed the old. Notice how your body wants to unwind, to move, and to undulate. Trust your senses in your root, as the shape shifting of the old transforms and releases constricted energy patterns. Notice your sensual nature as you unwind and get in touch with this energy and how it brings life to your body, to all your senses, and to your own awakened spirit.

Plant Spirit Medicine of Sacred Tobacco

Sacred Tobacco is the first plant that the Creator gave to the First Nations and indigenous, native peoples of the Americas. In Lakota tradition, White Buffalo Calf Woman brought the peace pipe and sacred tobacco, teaching the people how to purify themselves with tobacco, prayer, and connecting to the sacredness of all life.

In Peru, Sacred Tobacco is one of the most important plant medicines the jungle shamans and medicine people work with. In healing ceremonies, the shamans sing sacred songs, and offer prayers to Tobacco before they light it. Once lit, they blow the sacred smoke into the person needing healing, to clear Hucha, and to infuse Sami.

They also do the same to clear any space, home, or land. ***They never inhale it***, for it is only intended to be prayed with.

The plant Spirit of Tobacco wants you to understand his true spirit, who is powerful at sending prayers to Spirit, creating, and healing. The Spirit of Tobacco is a powerful male spirit who as an ally can do very 'heavy lifting' for you, clearing fear, trauma, and dense energy. He demands respect. If disrespected (such as unconscious use of cigarettes made with carcinogens, and the drawing the smoke into your lungs), Tobacco will kill you. He stresses the importance of truly knowing your allies, honoring them as yourself. In a sacred, respectful relationship, Tobacco will protect you and assist you in living in balance with Great Spirit.

Learning to work with Sacred Tobacco comes through sacred initiations and trainings. I began working with Tobacco more than 13 years ago first by receiving clearings and ceremonial blessings. A year or so later I began to pray with Tobacco, learning to use it to clear and to bless others. Next, I went to the Amazon jungle in Peru, and sat with Shipibo shamans in silence and prayer, in a dieta devoted to making Tobacco by ally. In this sacred ceremonial initiation, I actually spent seven days praying with the Spirit of Tobacco, as well as drinking a brew made from the tobacco leaves. This ritual and ceremonial work was like drinking fire, I must admit. Yet it brought me visions, cleared my physical vessel, and created a vibrational support system for me and all areas of my life. The Spirit of Tobacco is a powerful ally now since 2007. He teaches me something new every time we work together, as well as brings great protection.

The Shadow Medicine of Sacred Tobacco warns you to clear away any fears and addictive patterns, that separate you from the sacredness of Spirit in all life. Do you have an unconscious relationship with the substance of tobacco, devoid of any spiritual relationship? Have you disconnected from the spirit and sacredness of your relations and life experiences? Are you working to make money, but have lost the joy and spirit of what you do? Are you in need of an emotional and spiritual cleaning, so you can dream your life well?

Pray with Sacred Tobacco

Begin your sacred relationship with Tobacco by asking for his permission to connect, and then acknowledge his power of healing and protection. Ask Tobacco to be your ally. Thank him for his sacredness and for all he provides. Call upon the Spirit of Tobacco to purify your heart, and soul; to bring vision and support.

If you have access to pure sacred Tobacco (nicotine rustica from the jungles of Peru), gather it and place on your altar. Pray with it, but do not smoke it.

~ Sit with the Spirit of Tobacco, until he guides you to light a tobacco offering as smudge.

~ Offer prayers to Tobacco, as you place a small amount of sacred tobacco into a smudge shell or pot. Sit and pray with Tobacco as long as you are guided, in gratitude and respect. Ask Tobacco to assist you in creating a sacred, creative relationship to support you in cleaning fear patterns so you may clearing create with purity and love.

~ Then light in ritual.

~ Smoke yourself as you would with any smudge. Smoke your altar, and your physical space.

~ Sit in reflection and prayer with Tobacco, open to the guidance and healing energies.

~ Once the tobacco has burned out, prayerfully take the ashes and place on the corners of your land, or at the front and back doors of your home, onto the trees and plants. Do this as a ceremonial offering to the spirits of your land, in gratitude for all it gives.

When you are ready, ask Tobacco if you may put it into a sacred pipe to smoke. When guided, do so ceremoniously with prayer in similar manner as in the tobacco smudge ritual. Once you have prayed, light the tobacco, drawing it only into your mouth (but not into your lungs). Then blow the smoke to Great Spirit. Use to bless items on your altar, or creative projects, blowing the prayers and smoke directly onto the items. Use your intention in your prayer with Tobacco as to whether this is to clean and clear, to protect, or to create. Tobacco will do as you ask when you have a respectful and reverent relationship.

To go deeper in your relationship with Tobacco for clearing, I suggest training with a shaman or shamanic practitioner (preferably locally) who is adept at working with Tobacco as her ally. The shamanic path is one of continued initiation and apprenticeship. Find someone who is experienced in whatever you desire to learn. Always choose someone who is ready to empower you to be the knower through your experience.

Be humble as you call in powerful allies such as Tobacco. Call upon elders and wise ones who can create a safe place for you to have an experience and initiation. This also demonstrates respect for the shamanic heritage and lineage.

The Stone Spirit Medicine of Turquoise

Turquoise has been considered a master healer stone for many moons. It has been known to ward off danger, as well as to bring good fortune. In Native American traditions it has been believed that turquoise would absorb and transform negative energies, bringing great protection to the one who wore the stone. Others still believe Turquoise to be a stone of divination and knowing.

The green and blue energies of Turquoise bring the earthen elemental powers of both water and earth and are connected to illuminating the healing powers of the heart. It is well-regarded as a healing tool of purification, able to clear negative energies and adverse effects of human-made environmental toxins, such as EMFs. It has a calming effect, as well as one that brings higher conscious awareness to the soul.

This stone is one I always want in my medicine bag. Its magnificent healing properties are perfect on an altar, in a medicine bag, imbued into healing tools, and worn as jewelry, both for daily wear, and for ceremonial wear. Chinese fung shui traditions suggest placing turquoise in the eastern corner of a room to call in positive energy into your space, promoting well-being and good health.

Water to Clean and to Clear

Water is another excellent elemental ally for any healing ritual. Water easily cleanses your energetic field, even if it is an ordinary shower or bath with seemingly no magical qualities or intentions.

The Healer shaman calls upon the Spirit of Water's gentle, yet powerful forces to clean and to wash away. It isn't always convenient to immerse yourself in smoke, however for most modern folk, taking to the shower or bath is easy enough to do on a regular basis. A shower or bath is one of the most effective ways to cleanse your auric field.

Shower and bathe regularly to keep your energy field clean and clear, along with your physical body. Use the recommended Ritual Sea Salt bath, described below, up to three times monthly to detox your energy and auric fields.

The Ritual Sea Salt Bath

Sea salt baths are another excellent way to clean your energy bodies, giving you the opportunity for a complete energetic reset, spiritually, mentally, emotionally and/or physically. Sea salt is an amazing medicine of Mother Earth as it naturally extracts low frequency energies. When combined in ritual and ceremony, you will find a return to harmony, clean and clear, with greater life force and higher vibrations. This is the perfect detox to restore peace.

Sea Salt Bath Recipe and Directions

~ 1-2 lbs. bulk sea salt (Dead Sea Salt, Himalayan Salt, or other unrefined sea salt)

~ 1 cup baking soda (great for your skin)

~ 1 cup Epsom salts (relaxing and great for your physical body)

~ Optional: a few drops pure essential oils to relax (such as lavender, frankincense, chamomile)

~ Set your space for a time alone. Let everyone know not to disturb you for the next hour or so. Turn off your phone and other devices.

~ Light a candle. Burn incense. Lower the lights.

~ Set your intention for your cleansing, as well as your restoration and reset.

~ Play relaxing music or sit in silence, whichever you prefer. This is your ritual and ceremony!

~ Run your bathwater at a hot/warm temperature (not too hot).

~ Add sea salt, baking soda, and Epsom salts. Stir around with your hands to dissolve.
~ Add the essential oils to the back of the tub water. (Don't put under the running water, as it will break down the molecules of oil.)
~ Soak for 20 to 30 minutes, undisturbed.
~ Call your spirit allies to support you. Lift your prayers to Spirit.
~ Sit in silence, pray, or chant
~ Most of all relax. Open to receive blessings.
~ When done, lightly towel off, or air dry if you can.
~ Drink clean, filtered water before and after your salt bath.
~ Drink a nice hot cup of water with lemon juice or chamomile tea afterwards to continue to support your clearing.
~ If possible, go to bed, or relax with calming music or a book that lightens your spirit.

CHAPTER 6

THE ARTIST SHAMAN HEALER SAGE

WITHIN YOUR VERY BEING, LIVES THE WISE ONE

- Shamanic Medicine of Wisdom
- The Storyteller and the Sacred Clown, the Heyoka, and the Contrary
- Animal Totems Jaguar and Bear
- Plant Spirit Medicine of White Sage
- Stone Spirit Medicine Amethyst
- Silence, Darkness, and Reflection

The Shamanic Medicine of Wisdom - Awakening the Wise One Within

Awakening the wise, Sage shaman self comes with observation, experience, and reflection. This Wise One is naturally the ancient one, the old man or old woman, and the seasoned elder who has endured and grown through many experiences. Even if you are in a younger physical body, you can dance in the mastery of the Sage shaman self when you can stop, be still, and truly observe the fabric of any experience. The Sage shaman self understands the laws of nature and the laws of the Divine. She knows Spirit Law well and understands the rhythms and patterns of the flow of life. She is patient and lives well in the moment. This Wise One is also lighthearted and knows at the deepest levels of her being that All is Well. She easily transcends the foibles of human experience.

The Storyteller

Traditionally, tribal elders tell powerful tales to the younger generations to teach them and to preserve their cultures. Each time a story is told, it breathes life into the culture and its people while imparting important teachings that bring wisdom and power to the new generation.

A good storyteller digests her experiences of the Earth walk, no matter how difficult they were at the time. From this 'digestion' comes understanding and deep soul healing, nourishment, and perspective. The more dangerous and treacherous the experience and achievement, the greater the wisdom and the story.

Through many shamanic adventures, the inner storyteller and Sage wisdom begin to emerge within the practitioner. These shamanic adventures are often misadventures, bringing challenges, sickness, and shamanic death — the spiritual death of the false personality and ego. The human self often struggles, complains, and finds herself in a limited, lower-level human experience as the ego does all possible not to die. In this tempering process, the inner Sage shaman imbues the gift of tenacity to endure the difficult experiences. Ultimately, the practitioner emerges from the experience with the gift of wisdom and the ability to weave a wisdom story with many spiritual teachings to pass on to others.

The Sacred Clown, the Heyoka, the Trickster, and the Contrary

The Heyoka, or Sacred Clown, also known as the Trickster and the Contrary, all carry the shamanic medicine of satire to the point of blasphemy. This irreverent medicine has the power to shapeshift the circumstances by freeing everyone into laughter when at all possible, releasing patterns of ego and overly serious states of being. They are known to walk backward into a meeting of Chiefs and tribal leaders who are in serious discussions about one challenge or another, dressed in clown attire or that of the opposite gender. This trickster energy intentionally throws off the ego's self-important energy, deflating it and reminding those in power that they too are fallible and that power can corrupt if not aligned with Spirit.

Through the many shamanic adventures of difficulty and challenge, not only is the Storyteller born, but somehow, almost simultaneously, the Sacred Clown awakens. Laughter and humor surface to give perspective to the crazy and difficult experiences of the earth walk. This nonconformist perspective grants wisdom and a sense of freedom that lives outside of any rigid constructs of the norm.

Uzume
Katherine Skaggs © 2007

Since life is not what it seems, pay attention, as there will be times when the Sacred Clown and Trickster arrive to teach you to look at life differently than you have. Notice the fools in your life experience. They have entered into your awareness to get you to lighten up. They are here to help you remember that there is a larger soul experience taking place in the ordinary happenings of your life.

My favorite Heyoka clown story is about the Japanese Shinto Goddess of Laughter and Mirth —Uzume, and the great Shinto Sun Goddess Amaterasu. Uzume's powers of merry-making, humor, and dance saved the world when all was dark and dying.

*O*ne day Amaterasu, the most beautiful Sun Goddess, got mad at her brother, the Storm God, and marched into a cave and would not come out. The world went dark, and everything began to die! All the gods and goddesses were so upset that they gathered around a campfire, lamenting, crying, and wailing in fear. They had done everything to no avail, but Amaterasu would not come out of the cave.

Uzume, the lesser Goddess of Laughter and Mirth, saw the suffering taking place. Irreverently, she walked up in her clown-like nature, plopping her big drum down beside the campfire. She then looked around at all the chaos, stepped up on her big drum, and began to dance... and dance she did, sensually, dancing a bawdy and lewd striptease. Of course, she caught all the gods and goddesses off guard. With mouths draping open, they were captivated by this outrageous behavior and began to laugh. The more they laughed, the more outrageous and irreverent Uzume became in her dance. Everyone was drawn into an uproar of laughter, completely forgetting about their troubles.

Their mirth was so loud, Amaterasu could hear the gleeful uproar of the gods and goddesses. After a while, she could not bear that she was not a part of what was happening. She rolled the stone away from the cave door and emerged, bringing the light back to the land and bringing life back to the people.

If you have lost your light, it is time to call forth your Clown Medicine, your inner Uzume. It is time to laugh and to move into sacred merriment that you may release your fears and worries that you may lighten up! Call Uzume to bring lightness, joviality, creativity, and happiness that you may return to your childlike wonderment and potential.

Animal Totem Bear and Her Medicine

When I think of the Sage shaman self, I think of the wise one in the North of the Medicine Wheel, the place of within, of mystery, of winter and the depths of the night and Dreamtime. She carries the introspective powers of Bear Medicine, taking long winters nap, entering into Dreamtime to integrate and reflect.

Bear Medicine teaches the wisdom of rest, reflection, and restoration, going into hibernation when needed. Bear easily reflects upon its last adventures of the day or season as it goes into the restful state of Dreamtime. This state of reflection and restoration prepares her for a new cycle, so she may come out in Spring, ready to eat and play.

> Sage wisdom is the byproduct of being within the stillness and timelessness of dreamtime.

Shadow Medicine of Bear is here to remind you to stop, to sit down, to go within, as I can assure you that you have not stopped for a while. If for any reason, you have difficulty stopping, meditating, going within, and/or resting, you are indeed in the shadows of Bear. Without rest and reflection, it is challenging to gain wisdom from your last cycle of experience. Call upon Bear to help you find the strength and support you need to move within and to step out of linear time. Stop. Celebrate what you have created to this present moment. Breathe. Play. Take a break. Get a good sleep. You'll have greater clarity, perspective, and wisdom for the next round.

Animal Totem Jaguar and Her Medicine

Jaguar Medicine assists the Sage shaman self through the power of the darkness and mystery of the night, the inner spaces of presence, patience, and observation. Jaguar sits, unseen in the darkness of the night, in the perfect spot, patiently awaiting her prey. Completely still, she is effortless until there is a reason to move and to pounce on the opportunity in front of her. She wastes no energy and is fully empowered. Jaguar reminds you to be still and present, effortless and in no hurry, restful, knowing Spirit brings everything you desire, in the right timing.

The Shadow Medicine of Jaguar reminds you to stop wasting your energy, 'chasing your tail,' or stalking your prey when no effort is needed. When out of sorts with jaguar medicine, you may find yourself talking too much and not listening enough; you can't sit still and constantly want to do or to act, never resting. Most likely, you are avoiding your thoughts and feelings. You may be in a great deal of pain, spiritually, mentally, emotionally, and/or physically, as you have stepped out of integrity with your spiritual self. You have gotten lost in the outer, physical world of the earth walk.

If you find yourself in the shadows of Jaguar, it is time to be still. Go within through meditation, shamanic journey, and practices of self-reflection. This is where you will experience higher consciousness and Spirit's guidance. Sit in the dark of the night, in the stillness. Wait, watch, and observe both inwardly and outwardly. Find the optimal spot where you can view the activity of your outer world, as well as the activity of your feelings, emotions, and thoughts about everything happening in your world.

Black Jaguar Medicine
Katherine Skaggs © 2012

Breathe. Call in the power of trust to align within your being. Allow yourself to be fully present. Open to receive, for all is coming to you in the right timing. This is the experience of effortlessness. In this place, you will find true power.

Plant Spirit Medicine of White Sage

White Sage is well-known as a powerful plant medicine to cleanse and purify. It is one of my favorite sage plants to cleanse and purify everything from my home and sacred space to my body and shamanic tools.

The Spirit of White Sage, known as Grandmother to many, is known to go deep within the psyche and emotional self to release the troubles and fears one struggles with. Sit in ceremony and prayer quietly with White Sage, and you will hear her speak to you, loudly! She loves to communicate and will bring wisdom as you cleanse. The Spirit of White Sage is a teacher and healer who has much to offer. She is among the wisest of plant spirit beings.

As you move into ceremonial heart space with White Sage, observe her smoke, the patterns, the fragrance, and the energy she offers to clear negative energies, to calm the emotions, and to purify the physical and spiritual energies. She will bring clarity to your heart and mind.

Offer White Sage in prayer as a sacrament to the ancestors and your helping spirits. Ask her to carry your prayers to Spirit while clearing any difficult energies, emotions, and thought-forms. Open to her benevolence and be still so she can sing wisdom into your heart and soul.

Stone Spirit Medicine of Amethyst

The stone spirit medicine of Amethyst imbues many healing powers to the one who wears it or uses it in healing practices. Mystics, shamans, and healers have long understood Amethyst's intense beauty and power bring protection, calming of the mind, and spiritual wisdom.

Spiritual leaders have worn amethyst for eons as a symbol of wisdom and even royalty. Pharaohs of ancient Egypt wore it for protection from evil and misfortune. It was often worn as an amulet carved in the shape of a god or sacred animal. Ancient Greeks and Romans also wore it for protection and to think clearly in battle and business dealings. Christians wore it to signify the sacrifices of Christ.

To increase and to awaken your Divine heritage of spiritual wisdom, meditate or journey with amethyst on your third eye or crown, wear it in a pendant or some form of jewelry, place it on your altar, or in your medicine bag or shamanic tools. To enhance your dreams, place a piece of amethyst under your pillow before you sleep, focusing on your desires for wisdom and clarity of knowing.

The Power of the Night

Going into the Silence, Darkness, and Reflection

Go within the darkness of the night and the unknown of Great Mystery to access the deep, knowing power of the Sage shaman self. This is a ceremony and initiation to clean away the fear of the unknown and the fear of death.

The entire fabric of the shamanic practitioner is transformed through a near-death experience, an extreme illness, or shamanic death initiation.

> One must pass beyond the gate of fear to embody the wisdom of Spirit.

Ancient Egyptian initiations took their initiates deep into the darkness (and often into the bowels of the pyramids or other ritual spaces) where they had to face their fears of the unknown, possibly poisonous snakes or alligators in nearby waters. The initiation was to focus completely on their inner light, to connect to it as their anchor, their guide, and their shamanic magic and power. Adept focus on the energy of love and light was the only way to keep safe from the attractive energies of fear and fright. The reptiles could sense any fear the initiate held and would go after them. The greater their calm, the greater their heart space and inner light, the greater their ability to transcend physical danger. It was the only way to 'see' their way out of the situation.

Other shamanic traditions include the initiates digging their own graves to lie in, often buried up to their necks, in darkness from sunset to sunrise, where they would face their fears. The following morning the initiate would be unburied and washed ceremoniously. This cleaned the body and the soul, as the initiate released the ego's death and birthed the awakened consciousness.

You may never happen upon one of these initiations in this life. However, you can create your own night ceremony to release your fears and awaken your inner wisdom and light.

Star Lite Amora
Katherine Skaggs © 2011

The Ceremony of the Night and Darkness - Sunset to Sunrise

Begin in your own home, meditation room, or ceremonial space where you have an altar. Let your family and friends know that you are unavailable from night until the next day.

Preparation

~ Optional - to deepen your experience, fast during the day. Fasting can promote heightened altered states.

~ Optional - Stop drinking water several hours before you go into your experience. Hydrate well during the day if you choose to do this.

~ If you do fast - Have someone stay at the house who can be a 'watcher' to help you or provide assistance through the night. Have them sit outside of the ceremonial space but be available if needed.

~ Be prepared to sit in the darkness at night, to face your fears.

- Have your journal and a pen or pencil to record your experiences when the sunrise comes in the morning.
- Remove all external sources of stimulation, except the natural noises of the night.
- Cleanse and consecrate your space with white sage, prayers, and intentions to deepen your inner wisdom.
- Create a space where you can sit or lie down comfortably. Have blankets and what you will need to stay warm and awake.
- Make sure all electronics and sources of light are turned off as you begin your ceremony. Turn your electricity off completely if you can. (Have a flashlight if you need to go to the restroom.)

Ceremony

- Enter your space at sunset.
- Sit; pray; do your best to remain still and awake through the entire night. (Keep the lights off all night and all sources of light off.)
- Call in your spirit helpers, particularly bear, jaguar, and the Spirit of the North (night and winter medicine) to support you to go within.
- Still your mind through your breath. Breathe deeply to the count of seven, hold to the count of four, and breathe out to the count of seven. Do this over and over until your mind and body still. Use as needed throughout the night.
- Cultivate presence and stillness through your breath work and focus. Notice how your body wants to unwind and release energy as you move into the nothingness of the night.
- If your mind wanders to anything but light and love, move your attention to your heart center and the focus on love.
- A helpful mantra to center: "Nothing but love and light. Nothing but love and light. Nothing but love and light."
- To strengthen this focus, place your hand over your heart. Focus on the words as well as the feeling of your hand on your heart. Visualize the light of your heart bright and flowing.
- Come back to stillness, your breath, and your focus best as you can through the night.

~ When the sun rises, say 'hello.' Sit in the rays of the morning sun, soaking in the energy of your new cycle, clean, pure, fresh, innocent, and full of potential. You are reborn.

~ Journal and reflect upon your insights, gratitude, and wisdom.

These deep periods of reflection are an important part of the shamanic path that provide a deepening into your wise Sage self. If you can, explore this ceremony under the stars, in nature, in a safe place, do so. It will be well worth it to go into nature and the fullness of the night time.

Inner Shaman of Peace
Katherine Skaggs © 2011

THE MAP OF THE MEDICINE WHEEL

ANCIENT WISDOM FOR WALKING THE WHEEL OF LIFE IN HARMONY

Our Ancestors believed in the Medicine Wheel and the Circle of Life. When you fit one upon the other, you will see your world in its true form, releasing tears of joy as in ceremony. Everything has a rhyme and reason for doing what we did over countless centuries of honing and practice. It was living in sync with the natural processes.

- Tony Ten Fingers, Wanbli Natan, Oglala Lakota

The Medicine Wheel is an ancient tool for learning about the Universe and the sacred mystery called life. It is about our relationship and connectedness to all things, inwardly and outwardly, from soul consciousness to physical life. It is an outer expression of the cycles of Creation, representing conception, birth, growth, death, rest, renewal, cycles, power, healing, balance, and all rhythms of life. As a mapping system, it helps us understand where we began, where we are, and where we are going in our life's journey.

The human and the soul alike pass through seasons and cycles, dreaming, initiating, birthing, growing, harvesting, and dying in each experience. There is a constant evolution of the soul, the mind, the emotions, and the physical body in every breath. The medicine wheel reflects the wisdom of each course of the journey. In doing so, it assists us in consciously living life through purpose and intention. With practice, we may learn to live life as a purposeful adventure and a sacred ceremony of the soul.

Medicine wheels and sacred circles are used daily for prayer, reflection, and personal connection to Spirit. They were places to retreat for reflection. They provide a safe and holy container for rituals and ceremonies, opening and closing of events, projects, and ideas.

A physical medicine wheel is created by laying stones upon the earth in a circle. Place larger stones in each of the four cardinal

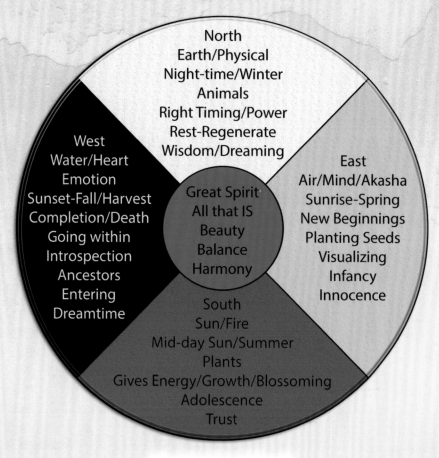

The Medicine Wheel

directions of the East, South, West, and North. Add one large stone or a smaller circle of stones in the center to represent Great Spirit. Power items or additional stones may also be added to the center to represent Father Sky/Above and Mother Earth/Below. Place smaller stones between the large stones to complete the circle.

The four directions are symbolic of the cycles of life, annually, seasonally, daily, and spiritually. The East is the place of sunrise and spring. It is fertility, potential, possibility, curiosity, planting seeds, birth, and childhood. The South is the place of the midday sun and summertime. It is adolescence, growth, blossoming, community, and heart-centered leadership. The West is the place of sunset and autumn. It is the place of harvest, completion, celebration, death, release, going within, introspection, stillness, and entering Dreamtime. The North is the place of nighttime and winter. It is the place of rest, regeneration, wisdom, dreaming, power, observation, and the right timing.

The four directions are the allies of Above, or Father Sky, and Below, or Mother Earth. Father Sky is the power of the Great Father, heavenly protection, wisdom, vision, the higher realms/dimensions of Divine consciousness, and Spiritual law. Mother Earth is the Divine Mother of fertility, birth, cycles, and death. She is the power of the natural world, its elemental energies, and the power of all of its creations. She is nourishment and blessings. She teaches us connectivity and relationships. She is our Earth Mother, who also bestows the powers of both creation and sacred destruction.

The center of the circle is where we recognize and honor Great Spirit and the place of the heart. The truth of everything extends from the center of the circle and is connected to all that is. Altars are typically placed in the center of ceremonies. This circle creates a safe and sacred container for the ceremony.

The Circle of Life and the Sacred Hoop

The Medicine Wheel is considered the major symbol of the Sacred Hoop of life, which symbolizes peaceful interaction among all living beings on Earth.

The sacred geometry of the Medicine Wheel is the Circle that symbolizes unity and never-ending, infinite flow. It is the symbol of oneness and interconnectedness. The Sacred Circle or Sacred Hoop is a Sioux concept recognizing that everything in the Universe is intertwined and in one continuous process of growth and progression. Creating a physical representation of this Sacred Circle, or Medicine Wheel ritually, with intention, creates a protected container or sacred space. Ceremonially calling in the directions of the Medicine Wheel sets up the energetic web, even if you don't have a physical construct. This, too, sets sacred space, imbuing protection, and clear boundaries. Consciously constructing the Circle or Medicine Wheel builds magical and spiritual energy for sending prayers and intentions with power. It is the ultimate place for ritual and ceremony as it opens a portal to Great Spirit and a place for all your guides, angels, and master beings of Divine light to support you.

White Buffalo Drum
Katherine Skaggs © 2012

Circles and spheres are known to energetically round out all communication, clearing edges and harmonizing flow. Circles create psychic boundaries and block the distractions and influences of the ordinary reality world, negative energies, and judgments of any others, physical or non-physical, as well as any other disruptive energies you don't want in your sacred spaces.

Working the Map of the Medicine Wheel

All Medicine Wheels are tools for teaching people about their place in the Universe, and their relationship to all things created by Great Mystery.

Over the years, I have found that the Medicine Wheel has offered some of the most profound wisdom and support for awakening. Every aspect of the Wheel provides guidance, direction, and understanding of my experiences. I can't pray enough with the allies of the directions. The conversation is part of my daily life, bringing wisdom to every experience. I encourage you to get to know the energies of this sacred circle of life. Pray with these allies. Work the exercises, and open to the spiritual power and allies that come through the practices.

~ Create a medicine wheel that is large enough for you to walk into and sit within if you have space to do so.

~ With intention, set a large stone in the East, the South, the West, and the North, making the four directions your anchors. Then fill in smaller stones around the four directions to make a circle.

~ If you don't have land or a yard large enough, set up your medicine wheel representation on an altar, no matter the size.

  • Use stones and/or power items to place in the East, the South, the West, and the North, anchoring each into your altar space.

  • Choose a sacred item that matches or represents each direction, such as owl in the West or bear in the North.

~ Add a sacred item that represents Father Sky and Mother Earth too.

~ At the center of your Medicine Wheel, whether on your land or your altar, place flowers or a smaller circle of stones or sacred items to represent Great Spirit.

  • Flowers are great to call in your spirit guides, allies, and Great Spirit.

  • Learn the powers and qualities of each of the directions. Then call them in, honoring them through gratitude for their power, gifts, and abilities.

~ Deepen your relationship with the powers of the Medicine Wheel by consciously working with each direction regularly in prayer and gratitude.

Even without any items in a physical location, you can visualize and invoke the medicine of the Medicine Wheel and its directions daily, as well as in ritual and ceremony, as you are called to do so. Every time you pray and invoke the Medicine Wheel and its allies, you expand its power and energetic web. Your attention, honoring, and gratitude constructs a protective and life-giving container for your prayers and dreams. Others begin to feel and sense the luminous energy, the more you engage with it.

Working with the Medicine Wheel will ground you into a solid foundation in understanding the weavings of life. It will teach you much about prayer, working with allies, and the power of consciously working with intention to create harmoniously and successfully.

Open a Medicine Wheel to set safe and sacred space before meetings, classes, ceremonies, rituals, shamanic journey, meditation, and all experiences where you want to be conscious and intentional in how you create. This is also a great way to start your day.

Remember to close the Medicine Wheel at the end of the experience, completing the circle, and releasing the directions. Everything you begin must come to an end. How you end something is equally important, if not more so, as to how you begin something. In doing so, you release the energy and experience of the event and can move to rest.

◊ DAILY NOTES TO SELF:

PRAYERS AND REFLECTIONS WITH THE MEDICINE WHEEL

Developing regular practices, such as daily prayer and reflection, is keys to living in harmony through the earth walk of life.

The practices given in the Daily Notes to Self sections assist you in building regular, supportive shamanic practices such as prayer, connecting to your allies of the Medicine Wheel, and quieting yourself through observation and reflection to obtain true wisdom. These are foundational practices that lead to mastery and intimate relationships with your soul self, your allies, and most of all, to Spirit.

As you enjoy the next chapters on the directions of the Medicine Wheel, you will learn how to call them as allies through prayer and daily practices. Imagine they are powerful Spirit allies who are always happy to assist you in creating your day, and your life with great power and awareness. Call to them in gratitude and reciprocity and you will build a strong ally who will guide you and support you. Honor each spirit in their powers, and you will indeed get to experience and know these powers in your life. Take time and practice calling to one direction, or to each direction daily and you will build relationships with these spirits of the Medicine Wheel, as well as understand how to build better relations in all of your world.

Open a Medicine Wheel to open your day, to open a ceremony or ritual, a class or event.

I like to use a rattle to invoke the directions as I call them in. Rattle to the direction you are calling in, and then motion the rattle to the center of your altar, or the center of the wheel.

For example:

(Rattle, rattle.) Spirit of the East, I call you now, with your pristine powers of the morning sunrise, and the fertile energies of Springtime. I ask that you open the Great Cosmic Void of potential and possibility, so I may plant my hopes, prayers, and dreams firmly that they may take root to grow. Thank you for your blessings of returning me to childlike wonderment and awe for how beautiful and good my life may be. Thank you for all you provide.

(Rattle, rattle.) Spirit of the South, thank you for your powers of light, of the Summer sun's warmth to grow my dreams into reality, of the Central Sun's soul light, to awaken my heart and soul. Thank you for illuminating my heart and my life. Thank you for opening my heart to living courageously. Thank you for the support you provide for all of my life.

(Rattle, rattle.) Spirit of the West, thank you for the powers of Autumn, and Sunset, the time of harvest, and death. I call upon you now to assist me in receiving the blessings of all the experiences of my day, and of my life, that I may be grateful and wise. Thank you for helping me to let go and let die what no longer serves me as I complete each cycle and each experience.

(Rattle, rattle.) Spirit of the North, thank you for the powers of the night and winter, the place of going within to reflect, to restore myself, to regenerate, and to return to dreamtime. Thank you for centering me in the stillness within, that I may know and be wise, that I may understand and integrate, that I may begin to dream with Spirit once again.

(Rattle, rattle.) Spirit of the Father Sky, and all the heavenly realms, thank you for the power of the heavens, the light above, and all around. Thank you for your powers of illumination and wisdom that protect and guide me upon my path. Thank you for assisting me in weaving a life on earth with the love, light, and wisdom of the heavenly realms.

(Rattle, rattle.) Spirit of the Mother Earth, dear Pachamama. Thank you for being the Great Mother who gave me my body, and the world of experience, filled with beauty, and all the cycles of creation. Thank you for the plants, and animals, the waters, the sky, the mountains, the valleys and all that you give. Thank you for guiding me on a path of harmony and reciprocity as I live in kinship with all creation. May all of life find the path of co-creation and respect, giving as we receive, receiving as we give.

(Rattle, rattle.) Spirits of this Land, thank you so much for creating a safe container for my day, and for all of my life. Thank you to the plants, the mountains and waters, the trees, the animals, the birds, and all of the spirits who visit, protect and guide me. Welcome to my day (or ritual or event). I thank you for all that you give today in how you support. May you too be blessed by the ritual of today.

(Rattle, rattle.) Dear Great Spirit, thank you for this dream of life. Thank you for assisting me in the path of waking up to myself as a conscious child of the Creator. Thank you for helping me and all of humanity find our way to greater harmony, hope, peace, and love.

Closing the Medicine Wheel

At the end of the day, or the end of a ritual or event, make sure to close the Medicine Wheel. To do so, say goodbye and thank you to the Spirits of each direction in reverse, beginning with Great Spirit, then the Spirits of the Land, Mother Earth, Father Sky, the North, the West, the South and then the East. Give thanks.

Yellow Seed, Child of the East
Katherine Skaggs © 2017

CHAPTER 7

SPIRIT OF THE EAST

Sunrise • Spring • Fertility • New Beginnings
Dreaming Anew • Infancy • Cosmic Void
Innocence • Curiosity • Childlike Wonderment
Planting Seeds • Courage
Purity • Innocence • Truth
Initiation • Leadership • Invention

The East is All About New Beginnings

The East is the cycle of the rising sun at the beginning of the day and the cycle of Spring within the year. It is a time of birth, creativity, inspiration, and welcoming the newness of any cycle of life. The East is also the place of great possibility, represented by the emptiness of the womb, the Great Cosmic Void, the un-manifest and the timeless. It is the innocence of the child and the potential of our heart's desires. Imagine! Anything is possible when working with the energies of the East.

The East is the Sunrise and the Morning Sun

The sunrise brings new light, awareness, and a new cycle. Greet the sun every morning, consciously connecting with this potent energy to super start your day. The sunrise is filled with charged particles of light, charging every part of your energy with pristine Sami. Use ritual at sunrise to connect with the potential of what has yet to come into form. Honor the energy of the East and the Sun to awaken the spiritual light within and the power of birth.

The East is the Great Void, the Cosmic Womb

The East is the Cosmic Womb, the place of the Akasha or the formless Great Void. It is pure potential and possibility. This fertile and formless place offers you the perfect womb to plant your heart and soul dream seeds. This space creates a safe and wildly possibly container for creating a new cycle, a new experience, a new dream. Are you ready for a do-over? The East will help you with that!

The East is Home to the Inner Child, Innocence, Curiosity, Imagination

Innocence, purity, curiosity, and imagination are the superpowers of the Inner Child and the East. Within the vast Great Void of possibility, lives the consciousness of the Inner Child who is constantly curious about how amazing her future can be as she dreams up fantastic adventures. When you arrive in the East, invoke the superpowers of your childlike nature, returning to the power of curiosity through a pure and innocent perspective.

How good can it get? When you drop into innocence, curiosity, and possibility, the quantum field, and the Great Cosmic Womb answer you.

The Universe must answer you as you ask. Focus the seeds of your desires through the power of the Child, and the Great Mother will hold your seeds and fertilize them, bringing them to form.

The Medicine of the East is Peace

When in the positive energies of the East, you are bathed in the energies of stillness, the sunrise that brings new beginnings, that elicits peace, serenity, tranquility, and the sense of oneness with all. You are centered in your readiness for new life, completely in trust that Spirit is guiding you. This complete trust brings high levels of peace on the path of new beginnings. You feel inspired and excited about the path that is unfolding.

The Shadow Medicine of the East is Chaos

If you are experiencing chaos, anxiety, destruction, war, despair, emptiness, and a sense of disorder in life while transitioning from one experience into a new cycle of life, you have dropped into the shadows of the unknown, the darkness before the dawn. Within the Great Void is vast potential and possibility, yet, it can be overwhelming when you have no idea of what to do or where you are going next. The only answer is to let go and to be. Any fear of the unknown creates chaos within the experience of the new beginnings.

When you become aware of the chaos and the anxiety, step backward on the Medicine Wheel into the North, to rest and reflect, or possibly all the way back to the West to the last cycle you just completed. When you complete a cycle of life, whether it be graduating from college, leaving a job, or getting a divorce, you need time to reflect and integrate your experiences to be ready to dream again.

It is important to harvest the good from your experiences. Then you can compost old identities and difficult experiences that cannot go into your next cycle. If there are experiences that you have attached to stories and old identities, old wounds, and outdated ways of being, they are most likely limiting your ability to move forward into new beginnings. Work with clearing exercises and releasing ceremonies to vanquish the past and any fear and limitations within these identities and stories. Finish anything left undone.

Then take a rest in the North for a while to integrate and to reset. Then you are better equipped to move into the East, fully rested, empowered to dream anew, and to enter the realm of possibility. Now, call upon the East to help you hold a positive focus on your goals, with peace in your heart that all is in Divine timing. Then you can trust that your future is clear and well-illuminated.

Air is the Element of the East

Air is the elemental energy and the spiritual aspect of potential and possibility. Air is associated with the Great Void, inspiration, imagination, creativity, and intellect. It is the foundational element of new life and all possibilities beyond anything you can imagine.

Air also connects the shaman to the power of the heavens, the un-manifest, and flight. Through prayer and shamanic journey, call upon the Spirit of Air to lift you above the earthly realm so you may see the potential and possibility awaiting you in your life from the perspective of Spirit. Then focus the power of Air through your intentions, your words, and your song to breathe life into the desires of your heart and soul.

Totem of the East

The Eagle is the totem for the East, bringing the medicine of Air and the messages from Great Spirit to guide all your creations. Eagle always brings the ability to see from a higher, spiritual perspective. Eagle also brings great strength and wisdom with its vision, assisting you in awakening spiritually through all you dream and create anew.

Feathers, seeds, and bird totems are great symbols of the East for an altar or medicine wheel, as well as anything that represents your hopes, dreams, seed ideas, birth, and childhood.

The Instruments and Sounds of the East

Om, according to Hindu lore, is the original sound of Creation. Life and all that exists is born of the sound Om. Every utterance of our voice sends sound waves into this world, creating vibrational patterns for our own experiences. Om is the perfect sound representing the East, the Great Void, and the act of birthing the world of possibilities through sound and intention.

Chanting the high vibrations of Om in meditation brings powerful creative forces into your prayers and intentions. Focus your intentions with the power of your emotions with your chant to manifest what you desire.

Bells, bowls, and chimes are well-known as the sound instruments used to call in the Spirit of the East. Use them in ceremony and ritual, whether it is a formalized gathering or your personal morning prayers. Doing so aligns your focus with your intention and prayer.

Honor the Spirit of the East as Your Ally

Greet the Spirit of the East as your ally of new beginnings, saying "hello" and "thank you" for all its power and potentiation it offers you now. Ask the East to bring in the new, to help you see everything in your life in a new light, with great clarity. Ask for your life to be filled with your greatest potential and for the East to teach you about the power of innocence wherever you go. Ask the East to help you see from the eyes and the heart of a child, with an attitude of great curiosity for the new and unexpected.

Vision Quest with the East, with Support of the West

A vision quest is a time when you step away from your everyday life, giving space to go inward into the sacred inner space of silence, disconnected from the linear world, fully focused on the guidance of Spirit. A vision quest is a ritual initiation into a new cycle of life. It requires great trust and courage to enter the Great Void in such an intentional manner. It is more than an afternoon meditation.

During this supernatural experience, the initiate seeks contact with the Divine, with the help of a guardian spirit, angel, or totem animal. Fasting, sensory deprivation, long periods of meditation, drum journey, and shamanic trance work may be used to invoke this extraordinary state of awareness. In some tribes and cultures, entheogenic plant spirit medicines such as peyote or ayahuasca may be used in ceremony to induce visions and awareness of the spirit realms.

In some tribal cultures, a vision quest is a rite of passage that young males take to ritualize entering adulthood. The rituals and practices vary from tribe to tribe. Historically, these ceremonies are led by elders and are supported by the young man's community.

The process includes a complete fast for up to four days and nights, alone at a sacred site in nature chosen by the elders for this singular purpose. During this time, the initiate is prepared through fasting from food and possibly water. Then he prays and speaks to the spirits for a vision and guidance. He asks for help to know the purpose of his life and the role he is to play in his community. He asks how to best serve Great Spirit and the people. Dreams and visions typically involve natural symbolism, such as animals and forces of nature, requiring the elders' interpretation. After the vision quest, the young person often apprentices or becomes a student of an adult who is a master of the role this one wants.

> Setting about your own vision quest is an honorable and mighty task, even if done in a modern-day setting.

Instead of beginning with a rigorous four-day fasting ritual, begin with shorter periods of time, starting with an hour meditation or shamanic journey, to a 24-hour time of silence and retreat.

Call upon the Spirit of the East and the West as your perfect allies for your vision quest. The East's powers to potentiate and give birth work concurrently with the West's death process to initiate you into a new cycle. Whenever you create anew, something always dies; consequently, death brings new beginnings.

Gratitude Practice to Begin
Your Vision Quest for New Beginnings

~ Set your intentions and prayers to create a new way of life.

~ Set your physical and energetic space through smudging, setting your altar, and prayer. Call in allies of the Medicine Wheel to set your space.

~ Specifically honor the Spirit of the East and West in how they can assist.

~ Breathe, drop a grounding cord down into Mother Earth.

~ Reflect upon and recall your blessings (of the past day, week, month, year, cycle.)

  • Take out your journal and write down the blessings that are of the most recent cycle. Admit and claim these so you can receive their energy and power.

Heart Chakra Shaman
Katherine Skaggs © 2009

- Reflect upon your relationships, your work, your home, your community, your spiritual gifts, your physical gifts, and so on.

~ Also, recall your blessings that have come from the difficult experiences that have tempered you and brought you to your knees. These are the tough lessons, full of opportunities to forgive yourself and others, to learn compassion, tenacity, courage, strength, and wisdom.

- Be grateful as best as you can, for these are the initiations that offer the greatest growth and illumination.

~ Now, write words of gratitude for the gift of every blessing you are aware of and have received in your life.

- Give gratitude to each person, place, and spirit you know were involved.

- Own the power of being here now, blessed, and in gratitude.
~ Reflect upon the courage and trust you have already embodied to create your life to this moment.

You have already created powerfully to be here now. As you recognize and claim your journey, you will continue to create with greater power and confidence. The gratitude practices also help you recognize the vast support that is all around you in the physical and spiritual realms.

A prayer of gratitude might be something like this:

Spirit of the East, thank you for opening new and vast possibilities to me at this time. Thank you for always being there to offer a new way, a reset, and a return to the power of purity, innocence, and creativity. Humbly, I honor all support and guidance that has come to me, supported me, and helped me create my life in greater peace and love. I am deeply grateful for my teachers who have come along the path, to open my heart, and to orient me to the Light and Love of the Divine. Thank you _____ (name each person you are grateful for who has blessed your path), and so many more in my life who have stepped in to bring light and to bring wisdom. Thank you to those who have been challenging on my path, whom I have loved but who have left, or whom I have left. You taught me boundaries, self-love, forgiveness, and compassion. Thank you, Archangel Michael, for always watching over my, protecting me, and guiding me. And thank you to all the Goddesses, Ascended Master, Angels, and Beings of Light who constantly guide and inspire me. I love and appreciate you so very much. And of course, thank you to all the animals I have ever had, have, or will ever have in this life, who have been there in unconditional love for me. Thank you, Lucky, so very much for your guardianship and old soul sage wisdom. You are a master, a shaman, a monk, and a wise guy for sure. Thank you, Desi, for being a special soul with great love and wisdom. Thank you, Sophie and Sadie, for always making me laugh and love more deeply. And to my dear soul friends, thank you for always walking beside me on this path. Thank you for the laughter, the tears, and the dedication you share with me, to be better, to be more loving, and to be full of light, not only for yourself but for all to experience.

This prayer is a short and simple example of gratitude. There is so much more I can write about, to be grateful for. Every life experience, no matter how good or difficult, is a place for growth and wisdom. As you reflect and find gratitude, may you be nourished, may your heart blossom, and may you feel comfort and peace.

Craft Your Vision Quest Experience

If you are not part of a native tribe with such traditions, you can fashion your own vision quest by taking a long weekend dedicated to silence and fasting. Begin with a 24- to 72-hour time to step away from your everyday life into your vision quest.

> When desire is born of your soul's purpose, it is a vibrational magnet to bringing hopes, dreams, and ideas into form for experience.

~ Turn off your digital devices, go into nature if at all possible, and remove all distractions from your world.

~ If you go into the wilderness, ask a responsible and grounded friend to be nearby, but out of sight, in the role of your Watcher. Your Watcher's role is to hold space for you to pray, to keep you safe, and to take you to safety if you need some sort of assistance. Your Watcher will also be the timekeeper as you enter into the world of Spirit.

~ Choose a place where you are safe both day and night.

~ Remove food and snacks and fast on water alone.

~ Set a circle space of 20 to 30 feet around your camp place as your boundary for the vision quest. Do not wander off. No hiking, as it can be a distraction. (Make sure you are physically healthy enough to fast for any length of time.)

~ Take a journal, a rattle, a drum, and the camping gear necessary to be alone in nature and the invisible world of Spirit.

~ Pray, reflect, sing, chant, drum, and rattle as you are guided.

~ Practice the grounding exercises and earthing practices.

~ Listen and watch for the animals, birds, and insects. What are their messages?

~ Be still. Open to Spirit's guidance, visions, and messages.

If you can't seem to find the 'time' for a quest of this length, take time daily to reflect. Early morning prayer time, sacred altar work, and nighttime prayers are all great places and opportunities to become still and go within. Take nature walks and look for guidance. Journey with the East and Eagle for vision. Do what you can to step out of your busy, linear, productive life. Build on the small time frames to open larger time periods where you can vision your life.

The East is the Ally for Manifesting Your Dreams

Learning to vision, pray, and focus your positive intentions regularly is the pathway to manifesting your dreams beyond anything you once could have imagined. The East is the perfect ally to assist you in consciously, intentionally creating what you desire.

Once you have identified your blessings, bringing to light the nourishment of having-ness already in your, it is time to focus on your true heart's desires. What do you truly desire?

When connected to the sacredness of your soul's creative purpose, Desire is the energy that draws hopes and dreams into manifest form. Desire for desire's sake can be the energy of lust and can ultimately leave you empty or addicted.

Your soul has incarnated to have the experience of its own creative consciousness through this world of duality. The good news is that you came with a perfectly encoded blueprint, also known as a soul map, programmed with specific desires, ideas, wants, potentials, possibilities, hopes, and dreams. When you focus on these soul desires, you give energy and weight to the dreams, creating synchronicities and the webbing of connection. This ultimately creates physical form, bringing you the experience you once only hoped and dreamed of.

Make sure to clear any fear that arises about manifesting your new dream, as it is a limiting energy that will distort your hopes and dreams. Fear either blocks the vision and dream or creates a fear-influenced version.

Dreaming the Future into Being
Katherine Skaggs © 2009

Write down your top five to ten desires, hopes, and dreams that are most important to you now. They may be something like change jobs, lose weight, remember my night dreams, write my book, get a new car, become more loving, take a class, manifest a relationship, improve my family relationships, get healthy, and so on.

How Good Can It Get?

Now that I have you wondering and dreaming about hopes, dreams, and desires, how much are you willing to receive? How big can you dream? How open are you to life being better and better and better? How fulfilled would you really like to be?

The Universe's secrets of manifesting work perfectly with the laws of quantum physics, all born through the curiosity and wonderment of a child. The innocence and purity of a child and her innate curiosity is the fertile ground for creation and the true vibrational power of the East. The Universe must answer your curious questions. Knowing how to ask the right questions assists you in drawing your desires into your life experience.

When I was in my mid-20s, I wanted to go back to school for art. I had already graduated with an undergrad degree in health and education and worked an unrelated job in advertising. I had wanted to go to art school earlier in my life and did nearly half a degree on the side already. Even though I had the messaging growing up that I was a great artist, there was always the overshadowing message from my father, "What are you really going to do for a living? Artists don't make any money."

At the time, I recall telling my boyfriend, "I would just love to go to art school for a year…if only I could." And he replied, "Why not?"

Yes, WHY NOT?!

With that, my imagination ran with it! Those two words were all I needed to hear to begin imagining myself painting, drawing, and creating. Within 18 months, I was at Kansas City Art Institute, where I spent three years, had amazing experiences, and achieved my Bachelor of Fine Arts degree in painting.

Along the way, I faced the negative messages and fear that once kept me from doing what I desired. I discovered that these messages and fears were far less powerful than the power of my heart and soul's desires. My inner GPS knew the way and provided perfect guidance, with amazing synchronicities to support me in receiving what I wanted. This made it all the more powerful to 'go for it.'

What do you dream of? What have you wanted for a long while now? Can you remember when you were a kid and day-dreamed of 'someday?' Do you still wish for a new way of life, a new job, a relationship, a move, a healthier body, and lifestyle?

What If and Why Not? Let's Dream Big!

~ Set a sacred space and container for you to begin to dream. Smudge. Sit at your altar. Light a candle.

~ Open the Medicine Wheel, calling in all of its allies and powers.

- Specifically, honor the Spirit of the East, as well as your Inner Child, and all associated allies and soul guides who are experts in connecting you to your true heart's desires.
- Ask for clear messages and assistance.
- Sit in wonderment and curiosity about all the aspects of your most important dreams you have identified. Reflect and meditate on your intentions to 'How good can it get.'
- Write questions about your hopes and desires that define "How good can it get…? What might it be life if…? How great will I feel when…? Why not go for it?"
- Write down your responses, dreams, and ideas. Use big paper, colorful pens, pencils and paints if you want. Make a statement that gives honor and energy to each. Draw symbols and imagery to express the energy and messages of your heart's desires as guided.
- Dream big, like a little kid waiting for the best gifts to open on her birthday! What are you excited to experience? Allow your curiosity to open the door to possibility and potential.
- Give space and time to daydream, allowing vision and curiosity to awaken the various aspects and possibilities you are drawing to you.
- Have a cup of herbal tea as you reflect and enjoy the possibilities. Create an experience of pleasure, fulfillment, and joy as you connect to your desires.
- When you feel complete, thank all your helpers for supporting you in manifesting your soul's desires.
- Close the medicine wheel and release your allies to go upon their way.

Face Your Fears

When you begin to admit your hopes, desires, and dreams, amazingly, it will begin to bring up any fear you have about not getting what you want…OR the fear of actually getting what you want! If this begins to happen, now is the time to clean into your heart, clear the fear, and to call forth courage to shore up and protect your inner child's innocence and wonderment for adventure and new life.

Notice, when you wonder how good it can get if you have any thoughts about how bad it can get if you change? Notice if you have worries and any messages of limitation that arise in your mental and emotional self. These negative fear energies are born of old messaging or negative experiences when things didn't go so well. The fear is now surfacing so you can face it for once and all, so you can let go of the old and heal.

Sacrifice Your Fears — Medicine Bundle Release

When fear arises, call upon the East to shed light on the wisdom from your past experiences and the Spirit of the West for completion and death in the old fear patterns.

~ Gather paper, pen, or pencil, a swath of red cotton cloth (6-8 inches squared), and a 12-14 inch red or black string or yarn.

~ Set your space to enter into a releasing ceremony. Smudge yourself and your altar, as well as your materials and surroundings.

~ Call to the Spirit of the East to illuminate and bless your dreams and soul desires, and to the Spirit of the West to clear away fear and old patterns that interfere or block your dreams and desires.

~ Through your breath or drum music, journey within to commune with this focus and identify any distorted Hucha patterns you would like to clear.

~ Release the words, story, and energies of the fear messages onto small pieces of paper, externalizing and exhausting the story and emotional energy. Also, add any remnants of the old, limiting experience to the bundle (i.e., a photo of your ex or a wedding band if you are releasing an old relationship so you can have a new, healthy relationship; an item from an unsuccessful business, such as a lease agreement, torn up and placed within the bundle, etc.)

~ Place everything you are releasing inside the swath of red cloth when complete. (Adjust the size of your cloth as needed!)

~ Place purifying smudge (any combination of sacred tobacco, sage, cedar, juniper, palo santo, or your choice of purifying herbs) on top of the writings inside the bundle.

- Add blessings of sacred corn, flower petals, incense, seeds, and other symbolic items that connote new life.
- Add sweetgrass to bring sweetness as you end the patterns that have held you back from your dreams.
- Place your hands over your bundle or onto your bundle, connecting your heart of gratitude to all you are releasing.
- Pray into your bundle, thanking Spirit of the West for clearing the old, and to Spirit of the East for bringing new life. Charge your offerings through your intentions and gratitude.
- Use smudge to smoke everything, for clearing and blessing.
- To complete your ritual, prepare a fire to release your bundle of old fear and to bring light to new beginnings.
- As you place the bundle in the fire, acknowledge that the past cycle is done. Speak it out loud, naming anything you are releasing as you like and if you like. Thank the Spirit of Fire for taking the old Hucha and transforming it into the restorative energy of Sami.
- Stand in the warmth of the fire, and soak in the energy as the fire expands through the release.
- Acknowledge the Spirit of the East and the void of possibilities that is fully open now, drawing your dreams into your reality.
- Thank the spirits of the East and West, as well as your guides and helpers.
- Stay with the fire until it burns down. Be present to the movement of the fire and the energy shifting. Honor your ritual transformation of fear into the energy of compost to fuel new life.
- When the fire is complete, as is your ceremony, speak out loud: "It is done. So be it. Aho."

Give Purpose to Your Desires

Once you have focused on your heart's desires, identify and write down your top five or so desires. If you can, sort them from what is most important to the least important. What are the esoteric and practical purposes and reasons for each of your desires? How does it serve your larger soul's experience?

Bless each item of desire through prayer and gratitude as you recognize its importance.

Create Altar Spaces and Dream Boards to Focus Your Attention

Take time to add items to your altar that represent your dreams and desires. Give them your attention through reflection, prayer, and blessings. Create a visual representation of your hopes and dreams through dream boards and other artistic representations where you pour your love, focus, intention, and attention through your hands. This brings your heart's qualities to your creative process and feeds the potential and promise of your dreams.

Take Action

Identify the action you need to take to bring your dream to earth in tangible form. As you work with wonderment and curiosity, what comes to mind when you think of an action that helps you put your dream into form? If you have a dream of writing a book, that is pretty easy. Write! And, as you know, that dream consists of much more than writing the book. What is the message and content of the book? What imagery and illustrations represent the messages of the book? Who is your audience? How do you publish, or who do you publish with? How do you market and distribute?

Asking these types of questions can help you get to the big picture of the dream and begin to see the steps involved in the dream's overall expression. As you begin to identify all the parts and pieces of your dream, your action becomes clear. This process weaves the invisible web that connects you to the support you need for your dream to manifest. Synchronicities and miraculous events begin to happen seemingly out of nowhere.

Slow down, do what you have the energy to do first of all. Take one action at a time. Everything unfolds over time, like a wonderful conversation with your best friend. Yet, it requires commitment and repeated action for any dream to come to fruition.

Ritual and Ceremony

Along the way, make sure to stay in the magic of ritual and ceremony, thanking the East and all your allies for assisting you. Do your best to work with the awe of childlike wonderment and the magic of dreaming big about how good it can get!

Give Your Hopes, Dreams, and Visions Your Love

Nourish your dreams similar to how you care for a beautiful garden full of the best foods you ever hoped to grow and eat. Stay away from poisonous pesticides and GMOs (worries, doubt, and fear). Put pure water (intention, attention, focus, blessings, prayers, ritual, ceremony) and fertilizer (compost from the old life released and let go) into the soil (mind substance.)

Weed your garden regularly (clear the fear of your mental and emotional blocks.) Use your shamanic practices to release and clear the fears. Use ceremony to bless yourself, your dreams, and your life.

Be patient. Never go dig your seeds up to see if they are growing, or you will destroy the environment they need for their perfect growth cycle.

Call upon the East as your master gardener ally. Always thank the East for bringing the energy of the new day, the dawn to your awareness, and your life. Thank it for using its power for new beginnings to bless your dreams and to show you the way for your visions. Thank the Spirit of the East for bringing you all you need to be in both the present moment and in the rhythm and flow of Creation. The East is a place of fluid stability. It is about being in the moment yet being in the flow of new life.

◊ DAILY NOTES TO SELF:

PRAYERS AND REFLECTIONS WITH THE EAST

Developing regular practices, such as daily prayer and reflection, are keys to living in harmony through the earth walk of life. The practices given in the Daily Notes to Self sections assist you in building regular, supportive shamanic practices such as prayer, connecting to your allies of the Medicine Wheel, and quieting yourself through observation and reflection to obtain true wisdom. These are foundational practices that lead to mastery and intimate relationships with your soul self, your allies, and most of all, to Spirit.

Good Morning Spirit of the East

Begin your day by honoring the Spirit of the East and the seeds of great possibility and potential that give birth to new beginnings for yourself and all of Creation.

Write a morning prayer to honor new beginnings in your Self, in your life, and your awareness. Make a welcoming prayer of gratitude.

An example of an East Prayer:

Good Morning Spirit of the East. Thank you for bringing in the Light of the new day. Thank you for supporting me in beginning anew, in my light, and the illumination of Spirit. I thank you for shedding light on my questions and desires. I thank you for illuminating my soul's path and guiding me into what is the most beautiful and joyful path. Thank you for this day. May I be a vessel of potential and possibility. Thank you for being my teacher and my guide.

Guidance from the Spirit of the East and New Beginnings

The Spirit of the East asks you to go within to the Great Void and open to your potential and all possibilities. This potential lives in the Great Void and without form or structure. This energy offers you all possibilities as you release any limitations.

Illuminating Your Potential and Possibility

Write down your hopes and dreams, imaginations, ideas, feelings, and desires. Admit them now and give them to Spirit in surrender to your highest and most wonderful good beyond anything you can imagine. Write down what comes to you without editing. Speak out loud to the Spirit of the East in prayer, particularly at sunrise, to release these energies to Spirit to be illuminated. Place in the direction of the East on the altar.

Identify Limitations that Come Up Regarding Your Dreams

Notice if any limiting thoughts or uneasy feelings arise as you admit your dreams, hopes, and desires. Call upon the Spirit of the East to assist you in illuminating any darkness that appears as you ask to bring light to your true heart and soul dreams. Allow yourself to write any beliefs or thoughts down, with your intention to release the energy that binds you from total freedom, power, and grace in all of your life, whether present, past or future. Do your best to bless any limitations with a compassionate heart.

Thank You, Spirit of the East, for Your Illumination

Focus on the Spirit of the East and its quality of illumination. Write a prayer to awaken the Light of illumination and new beginnings in your Self. If there are areas of your life that need illumination, ask the Spirit of the East to shine the light of new beginnings on that area and bring you awareness.

Here is an example:

Hello, Spirit of the East. Thank you for being my ally of new beginnings, potential, and illumination. Thank you for shining your light on me right now and hearing my earnest prayers. I appreciate the illuminating light of awareness and how you help me clearly see and understand my path. Thank you for shedding light on the answers to my concerns and areas where I need healing. Thank you so much for the potent energy illuminating my very potential and the possibilities for my dreams and hopes manifesting now. Thank you for being my teacher and my guide.

Any limitations that have appeared are energies that are stuck in time and space. They are the illusion of the mind and any part of you that has separated from the Creator and your own divinity. Compassion and forgiveness are the spiritual power tools for healing all trauma that has created the illusion of limitation and suffering.

~ Take each limitation, one by one, and wrap it up in a bubble of beautiful golden light.

~ Visualize the warmth and power of the light dissolving the limitations and energy of each illusion.

~ As the old pattern of limiting belief is dissolved, watch the golden bubble of light fill with the loving energy of your heart's desires.

~ Your body becomes warm and is activated in love.

~ The positive desire comes into form, is clear and bright.

Take time to acknowledge any new awareness, breakthroughs, and inspirations that come to you.

East Altar Work

Give Your Hopes and Dreams to the Spirit of the East

~ Place written intentions and prayers, along with sacred objects symbolizing your dreams, onto the altar in the eastern quadrant.

~ Thank the Spirit of the East and Great Spirit for taking your dreams and planting them firmly into the Great Cosmic Void.

~ Burn incense, smudge, and/or sacred tobacco to symbolize and experience your prayers being sent to Spirit.

~ Light a candle to represent the spiritual light that ignites the spirit within your dreams.

~ Inwardly watch the sunrise, shining the powerful light of a new day, a new cycle, upon your seeds, bringing them the warmth and the energy they need to grow.

~ Inwardly, or in spoken word, acknowledge that your dreams are happening now.

~ Sit in reflection, prayer, and meditation.

Entrust your dreams to the Spirit of the East once you have planted them into the Great Void. Bless them often, daily, and in ceremony and ritual when possible. Your seeds and prayers are now in gestation mode. Be patient and present, acknowledging this is done and will appear in right timing. In addition to blessing your dreams, notice what actions and synchronicities arise that support and feed your dream. Take action when it is clear what to do.

Work with the Spirit of the Child of the East, with the qualities of innocence, purity, and wonderment. Ask the childlike wonderment to well up within yourself, for the magnificence of birthing new realities, small or large. How good can it get?

Luminous One
Katherine Skaggs © 2020

CHAPTER 8

SPIRIT OF THE SOUTH

Midday Sun • Summer

Growth • Blossoming • Adolescence

Heart • Tribe • Trust and Boundaries

Generosity • Loyalty • Connection

The South Expands Light to
Illuminate the Heart and Grow Our Dreams

The Spirit of the South is here to assist you in opening your heart. It brings the energy of the Sun to Earth, joining with the water and soil of Mother Earth to give abundant life. The Sun is the heart of the Solar System and connects to the heart in our bodies. When we connect to the Sun, we set up a greater electrical frequency from our heart to our brain, from our Spirit to our body and personality.

The South's energies represent the container of the heart, which is a vessel for great light, and the foundation for great power. When the summer sun's light pours into an open heart, it provides nurturing, respect, protection, interconnectedness, and synergy with all life.

As we open to receive the support of this solar light, we can open to trust, innocence, and the fullness in our emotional selves. It also brings growth and expansion to every part of our world.

The South is the Cycle of Summer at Full Bloom

When we walk into the South within our own life flow, we find that it is the energy of beautiful plants blooming in the mid-day of the summer sun, bringing great color and abundance into our lives. It is the fullness of our hearts, and the blooming of our relations, our work, our family, and our joys. The midday sun's energy shines fully on our life, shedding light on all life we are creating. It is a well-tended garden of overflowing, nourishing gifts from Mother Earth.

The South is Associated with the Midday Summer Sun

In the Mexican Huichol traditional mythology, the Sun Spirit Tatawati comes to earth to illuminate our lives from our hearts outward. Tatawati brings great energy to all things within life, so they may blossom. This represents the fullness of the heart, pouring out and receiving back from its giving. The East's/Spring's seeds planted weeks, months, or years earlier come into form, into healthy experiences blossoming in your life.

~ Speak prayers of love and gratitude into a glass of water each day, then let it sit in the midday's sun for 15 minutes or so, soaking up the energy of the sun.

~ Then drink up while consciously and gratefully receiving the blessings of your answered prayers, filling your heart spaces with solar Sami and medicine from the ally of the South.

~ Imagine this wakes up your DNA. The light and warmth of the sun revitalize all your potential, all of your life, and all of your prayers into beauty and pleasure on Earth.

The Medicine of the South is Support

When in the positive energies of the South, you will feel supported in your life's journey. Your heart is full and warm, trusting of what is unfolding. You experience beauty, nourishment, and brightness in all life. You access your support system and know you have many within your circle who will go to bat for you, who are available to assist you or support you in reaching your goals. You feel the interconnectedness and blossoming, knowing you are part of a greater whole. You know Spirit always has your back!

The Shadow Medicine of the South is the Trap

If you feel trapped in any areas of your life — a relationship, a family, an organization, work, etc. — you are in the shadow of the South, unable to grow and expand, feeling no support at all. The once-protective and supportive container is small and limiting, leaving you to feel stuck, unsupported, and unable to access your resources. Your heart is closed, and you cannot feel the oneness with life.

Stagnation, complaining, and victimization are symptoms of being trapped in your thinking, your feelings, and your life experience. To release the stagnant energy of the trap, you must find a way to move the energy.

Resetting your focus to solutions and possibility is crucial to shifting. Set an intention to shift up and out of the trap. Focus on gratitude for what you have as well as on what you desire to create. Find an action or movement to release stuck energy and to open to flow. This might be to sit and drum for 10 to 30 minutes; or to stand tall, open your arms as wide as you can with shoulders pulled back, looking upwards to the sun; or to lay face down on Mother Earth for 20 minutes to release into her all that is stuck. It also may be a staccato dance movement to shake away and drop stuck energy.

Here is an example of a visualization you can use to open your heart:

~ Sit in the noontime sun, stretching your arms fully open and outward, allowing the Sami of the sun to bathe you in warmth.

~ Focus on your breath.

~ Focus on the sun and the intention to breathe the sun deep into your heart.

~ Breathe in sunlight and warmth to a count of seven, hold for a count of four, release to a count of seven.

~ Do this for 10 to 15 breaths or until you feel a shift.

Fire is the Element of the South

The summer sun and the element of fire are the perfect energies of the Spirit of the South. They warm the soul and illuminate the authentic heart. Their solar fire purifies and lights up the heart center and emotional body, bringing growth and expansion to all that is illuminated. This powerful energy animates and nourishes us from the very core of our beings. As our heart is purified and filled with light, we become more open-hearted, courageous, and emotionally harmonious.

~ Call in the element of fire and the Spirit of the South.

~ Imagine the golden light of the summer's full sun, penetrating and purifying your heart, burning away old stuck energies that no longer serve you.

~ Say "thank you" to the Spirit of the South and fire for regenerating your body, mind, and soul.

~ Bask in this warmth, allowing your entire being to relax and reset in the light.

Totem of the South

Animal totems of the South represent passion, courage, strength, fertility, and nourishment. Lions are a perfect example of a South totem, representing the power of the heart, courage, and leadership.

The Instruments and Sounds of the South

The low beat of the drum returns us to the heartbeat of the Mother Earth, to our own mother's heartbeat, and to the heartbeat of humanity. It opens our hearts and awakens our inter-connectedness with all life. It is primordial and grounds us to our place on Earth.

If you ever find you are in the shadows of the South and need your heart opened, sit and drum for 10 to 30 minutes to clear your energy and to open your heart. If you don't have a drum, play some shamanic drum music to return home to your heart and your sense of connectivity to life.

Honor the Spirit of the South, as Your Ally

Thank the Spirit of the South for its power to illuminate, to bring growth, and to awaken your heart as you connect to it as an ally. Through your heart center and humble gratitude, ask the Spirit of the South to bring into fullness the seeds you have planted during the Spring.

Align your heart as the vessel of the summer sun's brilliant light. Then shine the light brightly into your world, to bless, and to bring growth and expansion.

Ask the South to teach you about the power of your emotions when held in this bright light. Ask the Spirit of the South to teach you about your interconnectedness to all life and how you can live from the heart space in every part of life, honoring all beings, as yourself. The South is a visible, external container of the heart.

◊ African Lore and the Medicine of the Sacred Heart

In African shamanic lore, each chamber of the heart has a purpose and meaning in walking the shamanic path of life.

The Clear Heart

The upper right chamber of the heart is that of the Clear Heart. The Clear-hearted person is trustworthy and safe. They are clear in their expression and true to their words and actions.

If the Clear-hearted person falls into the shadows of their true being, they experience confusion because they serve two gods. They stop trusting Spirit to take care of them. Instead, they serve the god of the false personality or ego. They manipulate themselves or are manipulated by others.

The Whole Heart

The lower right chamber is that of the Whole Heart. The Wholehearted person does the best she can, staying open and giving her all, no matter what. The Wholehearted person follows her bliss and her passion, always fully committed to her heart's desires.

When in the shadows of this expression, the Whole Heart becomes the Half Heart. A Half-hearted person is lazy, half-hearted, and uncommitted. The Half-hearted person also serves two masters — the false personality pitted against Spirit. Fear of commitment, not being responsible for what happens, and having a foot out of the door are some of the Half-hearted person's ways.

The false personality loves to use distraction to distort the Whole Heart's energy as it moves into the Half Heart. Walking the shamanic path supports you in facing the distractions and the illusions within human life so you may choose consciously what you truly want. Then you are free to create the life that you desire by persistently and relentlessly choosing what is in alignment with your soul's desires. The shamanic path is an honest path of the heart. Be assured that the false personality dies more and more as the heart leads the way.

The Strong Heart

The lower left chamber of the heart represents the Strong Heart. The Strong-hearted person is not afraid to show how they really feel. They stand up for their beliefs with courage and confidence. They are warriors of the heart and lead only with their hearts.

The shadow of the Strong Heart is the Weak Heart. Weak hearts are full of fear all the time and express themselves in a cowardly way when it comes to what they want. They become small, inconspicuous, deflated, and lack importance in their worlds. They often hide from who they really are and are self-deprecating. They lie to themselves and to others on a regular basis because they are cut off from their real heart feelings. The Weak Heart is often led by the false personality rather than by Spirit.

Be true to your heart's desires, and you will find the strength, courage, and confidence to be the Strong-hearted person.

The Open Heart

The fourth chamber of the heart is the Open Heart. Open-hearted beings are very creative and open-minded, full of spontaneity, and open to Spirit's guidance. They are inviting, connected, loving, secure, and compassionate.

When falling out of the Open Heart, one becomes the Closed

Lioness Heart
Katherine Skaggs © 2018

Heart. The false personality convinces this person through fear to be rigid, stubborn, selfish and closed to love and the potential the world is offering you. This fearful way may even make you a zealot and unable to look at the ways of others offered to you. This can produce judgments, disappointments, resentments, anxiety, victimization, restlessness, and a lack of satisfaction.

Work with practices of compassion and forgiveness to keep your heart open. This will allow the fluid and flexible energies of the Open Heart to be fully alive and expressed.

Healing the Wounded Heart

The shadows and wounds of the heart are all expressions of fear, created by the false personality. The fearful unconscious patterns of the false personality control our lives and keep us asleep. These fear patterns are rooted in the stories the false personality loves to tell again and again. Repeated stories of fear hold us hostage in an energetic loop of destructive patterns.

The way to heal these shadows is to first face the wounds with compassion, honesty, forgiveness, and love. We must be honest with ourselves about what we are experiencing to open to receive the healing. If we are not honest with the hurt, the pain, and the fear in the story, we cannot change, and we cannot open to receiving support to shift the energy and experience.

Ask the Spirit of the South to shine the light of compassionate truth and unconditional love upon you, to assist you in releasing false beliefs and the deadening stories of wounding. The stories are the distractions that keep you from healing.

Exercises to Awaken the Heart and Heal the Wounds

Again, with the support of the West, we will work to strengthen the power of the South and the Heart medicine we each carry.

What stories do you tell over and over of who you are? Of what your situation is? Of how you are not happy? Where do you find yourself saying, "They did this to me, he did this, she hurt me, etc."? What words disempower you, reflecting a fractured self-image or life experience?

~ Set your space for deep inner work. Go to your altar, meditation room, or a safe space in nature conducive for this work.

~ Smudge. Call in the directions and all of your allies to support you. Thank the Spirit of the South for its power to heal the heart.

~ Play drum music or meditation music to move into a calm, centered space.

~ Focus on one of your stories of heart wounding that you would like to clean and clear from your heart.

~ Imagine the story as a movie or play, and that all the people involved are actors.

~ Imagine these actors in your movie are actually soul friends, playing out an experience for your learning. Put them all in a bubble of pink light as you do this.

~ Place them in front of you on the stage of your imagination.

~ Identify their roles and the ways you felt wounded in your experience.

~ Write everything in full detail onto paper. Face it, and then let it go! Write out all you have to whine about and let it go onto the paper.

~ Put color to it. Put symbols to it. Paint the feeling of it.

~ Let it all go onto paper and release the story in full expression!

~ Now, step back from the story. Imagine yourself from above and that all the players are you. You have created everything!!!

~ As you reflect, imagine that you can, from this perspective, recognize the imbalances, the injustices, the attitudes in your thoughts, and your heart.

~ Good news! You are the author, the artist, the dreamer, and the director of your life's situations, so you can edit every part through forgiveness!

~ Breathe. Center into your heart.

~ Now look into the eyes and hearts of everyone involved and ask their forgiveness for any suffering you might have created in this story.

~ Breathe. Breathe in light and compassion. With your breath and your imagination, fill your heart with the light of the sun and Spirit.

~ Then blow this light into each player with compassion and unconditional love.

  • Visualize them returning to wholeness.

  • Thank them for teaching you about wholeness, love, compassion, forgiveness, and acceptance.

  • Send them blessings and release the story, as if it were a balloon flying off into the heavens of Great Spirit.

~ Breathe. Connect to the sun again, breathing in the light, warmth, and the compassion of unconditional love into your heart, overflowing into your physical body, all of your energy bodies, and your soul.

Can you see from another perspective? Are you willing to be the creator of this story and to choose how to change it with love? Can you create a new story that is full of transformation, learning, and acceptance? Can you imagine a different way?

~ Take your old story and put it on your altar in the quadrant of the South or the West, your choice. Trust your intuition and guidance.

~ Then ask the Spirit of the South to open your heart with its powerful light, clearing your heart of all Hucha of this story and any other story that limits your ability to be loving and receptive to love.

~ Ask the South to show you that you are interwoven with all life, and to these players of your dream.

As you release and forgive, you may now dream well, with a Strong Heart, an Open Heart, a Clear Heart, and a Whole Heart.

Another Heart Exercise to Awaken and Heal Yourself and Your World

Begin with focusing on the feelings of appreciation and gratitude, without any reason to do so. Be grateful just to be grateful and get in touch with that feeling.

This creates a vibratory state that balances your brain/mind/emotions/body and helps you access that state at will. As you cultivate this, you will find you are less apt to go out of balance when the world around you seems chaotic and perhaps even frightening to most. You will discover that you will be centered in this energy, and it will help you draw in more peace, gratitude, and beauty to you.

~ Once you are masterful at being in gratitude, expand your focus by putting attention on your heart.

~ Focus on your physical heart and surround it with the feeling of love and gratitude.

~ Visualize a beautiful magenta pink energy around it and through it. Imagine this pink light is the vibration of love and gratitude.

- Send it to the cells and tissues of your heart.

- Imagine it floating into the spaces between the cells.

- Expand this light outward, entering into every cell and between every cell in your physical body, as well as your energy bodies.

- See this energy expanding until you are surrounded in a beautiful, luminous bubble of light.

- Then, with your intention and your breath, expand the light into your home, then your community, then your city and state, then across your nation, until you see it radiating around the earth, and then into the cosmos.
~ Practice regularly to expand your state of peace, bliss, or even ecstasy.

Expanding into this energy vibrationally protects you from the lower frequencies of fear, whether it be that of friends or family, the people at the grocery store, or that of the mass consciousness of the world at large. This frequency also magnetizes all that you need and desire to support you in the transitional state of our species and our planet. Your gratitude-oriented vibratory field will shape-shift not only your attitude but will awaken your very DNA. You will be the transformer of everything around you as you live in this high-frequency state of love and gratitude.

Working with the Power of the South to Move through Transformative Times!

Just as the Great Mother Earth has been realigning her body through earth changes, be confident that you, too, have been transforming through the powerful energies of these times. The increase of earthquakes, tsunamis, tornadoes, and volcanic eruptions are reflective of the meeting of the higher frequencies and the lower frequencies on this planet. These robust energies are breaking away the old patterns that cannot move into our future.

Many old and hidden ideas, beliefs, and ways of being are being exposed, so they may die, both personally and collectively. Just as the Earth Mother has been under incredible change, so have our energy bodies, our physical bodies, and our lives. These energies are ultimately beneficial, yet their intensity may cause you to feel as though you are having a breakdown, mentally, emotionally, or physically. The good news is that you are in a wonderful place to leave the old dis-harmonious patterns behind and move into new ways that bring greater harmony, joy, and wisdom.

Personal Responsibility

The changing times are calling each of us to take a new level of personal responsibility. No more victimization! If you are the one dreaming your reality, then you are responsible for your outlook and your response to everything. When you accept this, you naturally drop the belief that anyone can take your power or harm you. In the process, you take your power back. It is time for you to stand in your own truth and become free of false outlooks and systems that are not aligned with your true heart-knowing. Get in touch with what you truly desire and begin there.

If you are in a relationship, job, or situation that no longer serves you, admit it! Ask Spirit, your Higher Self, guides, and angels to assist you in letting go of the addictions to pain, suffering, and lack, etc. Ask them to guide you into courage, confidence, self-love, and trust that you can move toward what you desire and receive it. Recognize when you feel out of harmony. This is your power drain. Ask yourself, "What is the shift to harmony?"

Taking responsibility begins with honesty with yourself. Discovering areas lacking harmony takes courage. Yet, once you have admitted what is out of sorts, you begin to find your power in choosing more love, more respect, more honor, more joy.

As you take responsibility for your situations, recognize it all begins within. It is not the other person or the other situation causing you distress or lack of harmony. Examine your point of view and strong emotions. What judgment, fear, sadness, resentment, frustration, and anger do you carry? What are the stories you tell yourself about the situation?

Read this again! It begins inside of you. How you think about, feel, and respond to the outer circumstances reflects your own attitude and stuck-ness. Once you recognize this, you can unhook from the negative imprint of these attitudes and feelings, moving out of duality into a space of neutrality. Focus on compassion for yourself and your experiences. Then they have no power over you anymore.

Admitting you need change is the first step to shift! Admit what is wrong or out of order as the first step to restoring happiness.

◊ Daily Notes to Self:

Prayers and Reflections with the South

Thank You, Spirit of the South, for Illuminating My Heart

Offer your prayers, affirmations, and gratitude to the Spirit of the South for bringing light into your heart for healing, awakening, growth, and support.

Here is an example of a prayer to the South:

*H*ello, Spirit of the South. Thank you for being my ally of the heart and of amazing growth opportunities. Thank you for shining your light on me right now and for hearing my earnest prayers. I appreciate the illuminating light of awareness and how you help me clearly see and understand my path. Thank you for shedding light on the answers to my concerns and areas where I need healing. Thank you for being my teacher and my guide.

Write a prayer asking the Spirit of the South to shine vast light on your soul's heart so you may know your wholeness, so you may awaken your DNA, so you may grow wise in the teachings of the

Heart, and so you may know the support that Spirit offers you in the worlds of the seen and the unseen. Where do you most need to light up your heart?

Light a candle each morning to symbolize the light of the Central Sun and summer's midday sun.

Guidance from the Spirit of the South for Expansion

The Spirit of the South always encourages you to trust your heart, to follow your heart, and, most of all, to keep the light bright within your heart space, as your heart is the guide to living in balance. Work with the Spirit of the South and the light of the Central Sun to illuminate your path and to hold the space for all your dreams to expand through the powerful energies and light of love.

South Altar Work

Call the Spirit of the South to Illuminate the Power of the Heart

The most powerful force of the Universe is unconditional love. It is high vibrational, illuminating, and transformational energy. Work with the ally of the South to awaken the light within your sacred heart and to grow your dreams.

~ Smudge your altar and set your intentions.

~ Light a candle to honor the South and the Spirit of Fire.

~ Place rose quartz and other sacred objects representing the heart, tribe, support, and illumination onto the southern quadrant of the altar.

~ Honor the Spirit of the South, along with the spirit of each sacred item that is here to assist you now. Thank them for taking your prayers to Spirit and for helping you now.

~ Offer gratitude with smoke and spoken words.

~ Speak or focus on your prayers and intentions with the South, and the helpers of the South to support you now, for opening the heart, for keeping your dreams safe, for expanding love through your awareness.

~ Chant, sing or hum the sound of 'AH' to open the heart.

~ Visualize green and pink light around you and through your heart.

~ Drum, drum journey, trance dance, or meditate to drumming music as you sit in the South and call your allies to support your heart dreams.

~ Be still, receptive, and focused inward on your heart space until you feel completely grounded and present in your body again.

Crow Woman
Katherine Skaggs © 2007

CHAPTER 9

SPIRIT OF THE WEST

Sunset • Autumn
Harvest • Completion • Celebration
Death • Release
Going Within • Introspection
Home of the Ancestors

The West is About Harvest, Endings, and Death

The Spirit of the West brings harvest, endings, celebration, change, and death/transition. With the power of introspection, we can begin to understand and integrate the experiences of our life, what our lessons have been, and what we need to let go of to continue our learning. The West also opens the portal to the wisdom of our ancestors. This is the place where we honor our ancestors and ask them to come teach us from the dreamtime.

The West is the Death of
Summer and the Arrival of Autumn

The season of the West is Autumn, a time of gentle change brought about through turning inward. This is the time to harvest the rewards of our hard work that have come in our two previous cycles of the East and South. It is time to enjoy the fruits of our labors, and to also let go of all that has completed and is returning back to Mother

Earth. The West is the time to prune the baggage of our lives, and to let go of anything we don't want to bring into our next cycles of dreaming, creation and experience.

The West is the time of maturity and late adulthood. It is the time of Fall, the time of the setting sun, the time of twilight. The daylight fades and brings a new awareness in this time of gradual change. When the darkness comes we must be courageous so we may look within to find the light. We may be challenged to understand what is Spirit and what is fear as we peer into the darkness. The West encourages you to look with eyes of your illuminated heart so you may better distinguish what is real and what is only the shadows born of fear.

The West is the End of the Day and the Sunset

As we complete the cycle of another day, we are encouraged to sit with the Spirit of the West and the setting Sun, placing anything on the altar that we need to give up to Spirit… any worries, any endings, anything we need help with, give it up to Spirit as the day ends and trust Spirit takes care of all things.

The Time Period of the West is the Present

Our future is created by the beliefs that we hold in the present. Changing those belief patterns changes our future. Use the time of the West to become still, mindful and present.

The present time is the only time
we can invoke change.

The Medicine of the West
Courage and Clarity of Intention

When you are positively aligned with the West, you feel good about yourself and your life experiences, regardless of their ease or difficulty. You can easily reflect upon your life passages to date, harvest the good, and then courageously let go of the past and all of its baggage. This includes people, identities, work experiences, accidents, tragedies, and all else that is outdated and cannot go forward with you, without regret. You are fully present, grateful, and accepting. You can accept the value that you have received from all the experiences of your life. You are clear about your intentions and ideas, and what to proceed with next.

The Shadow of the West
Fear, Obsession, Stuck, Attached

If you find yourself unable to let go of the past in any way, you are most likely stuck in the fear-born darkness and shadow of the West. You may be obsessed with an ex, stuck in a story, attached to a problem, or even identified with an old identity, such as the head of your class in college. Your past haunts you in every way you can imagine, and it seems you just can't move forward or let go.

~ Set your sacred space at your altar, or in a place where you can move into ceremony to let go of fear.

~ Smudge and smoke your space. Set your intentions to be let go of the past and to move fully into the stillness of the moment, into present time.

~ Call upon the Spirit of the West and the medicine of death to clear all fear and past patterns that you are stuck in. It is time to let die what needs to die.

~ Take stock of the good that has come from the past. Admit and harvest the good! BE PRESENT to what is.

~ Call the Spirit of the West and Owl to clear the fear, and to compost the old.

~ Then identify everything that needs to die — name what is outmoded, long over, stagnant, not working, and out of date —all people, events, jobs, relationships, and things. Release out loud into prayer, or onto paper.

~ Light a fire in your fire pit, cauldron or fire safe container, thanking the Spirit of Fire for its powers of transformation.

~ Release your written words and spoken prayers into the fire. Let go. Let the fire, Owl and Spirit of the West consume the old.

- ~ Release doubt and all questions of what was or what will be into the fire. Surrender all to Spirit.
- ~ When you feel complete, honor that it is done by saying out loud, 'So it is. This is complete. I am complete. The past is released and I am 100% present in the now moment. I am nourished by all I have and all that I am. I create my dreams only through love. Aho.' (Or something along these lines in your own words.)
- ~ Breathe in trust. Do your best to honor that 'All is Well.'
- ~ Breathe. Focus on being present. You are free.

Water is the Element of the West

The element associated with the West is water, bringing the energy of flow, movement, dissolving boundaries and holdings, cleansing, and healing. Water is also the element associated with the emotional body, the subconscious, the intuitive, the sensitive, the empathic and the creative. Go deep within your inner waters and your subconscious self to access introspective spaces and depths of your true self, then ask the waters to help you flow through any attachments and wash away fear and limitation.

Totem of the West

Owl is a powerful totem of the West offering healing and illumination. Owl is considered the Night Eagle, and is the one who can

see through the darkness of illusion of the ego. Owl is said to have golden eyes, representative of the Christ light, bringing the illumination required to 'see' clearly in the dark. Owl's wings allow owl to fly silently through the night, unseen by the other creatures. In doing so, Owl brings the medicine of silence and discernment, and of knowing when to be seen or not.

Owl is a powerful healing ally, as it eats the Hucha that holds patterns of discord. Call on Owl to clear away old attachments and fear patterns born of the past. In the process, Owl helps you become free! Count on Owl to assist you in seeing more clearly the truth of any situation, as you also discover the wisdom Spirit offers you for every experience.

Anytime fear seduces you from moving forward in your life, call Owl and the Spirit of the West for assistance. Be lifted up on the wings of Owl medicine to see beyond the illusions of ordinary reality.

Those who carry Owl medicine are often shamans, healers, sages, and medicine people.

Instruments of the West

The didgeridoo, clicking sticks, and clicking stones are the sounds of the West. These instruments are powerful vibrational sound tools for releasing the deepest fear and trauma patterns that are physically set into our bones, as well as in our energy bodies. These high-frequency instruments break away distorted patterns and imprints that were created through experiences of shock, fear and trauma. These imprints may come from carry-over trauma from past lives, ancestral trauma patterns/frequencies carried in the bones through the genetics, and uncleared trauma from current life events and accidents.

Clicking sticks, clicking bones and clicking stones represent the bones of the physical body. In the shamanic body mapping system, the bones are the physical expression of the patterns of our experiences, and the experiences of our ancestors. When we have fearful experiences, shock and trauma, these patterns can become lodged not only in our energy, but may be imprinted at a deep genetic, physical level. If left unattended, this trauma can manifest at some point into dis-ease and illness, or a broken bone.

Breaking a bone, which you obviously do not want to do, is an unconscious attempt to break a pattern. Instead, click together sticks or stones through your energy field and around your physical body, especially in areas where you feel stagnation. This break up stuck and distorted energy patterns, resetting you into higher frequency patterns of harmonious life-giving energy.

Make Your Own Clicking Stick, Clicking Stones or Clicking Bones

If you would like to try this yourself, you can begin without any expense at all. Go on a nature walk and ask Spirit to show you your sticks or stones, or even old bones upon your walk. This may take several walks to find what you need to create your clicking sticks. Two sticks or two stones or two long bones that fit easily into the palms of your hands are excellent for creating your healing tools.

For your clicking sticks you can use sturdy sticks that come from the limbs from any tree. You can also go to the hardware store and buy a dowel rod that is ½ to 1" in circumference. Cut the dowel into two 10 or 12" rods. Sand, carve and/or paint your sticks as desired. Voila! You have a beautiful set of clicking sticks.

For a set of clicking bones, find a long bone, which is a shaft with two ends. A dried femur from a wolf, coyote, elk or deer are perfect. Use as is, or paint with symbols as you desire.

To create clicking stones, choose two rocks large enough to fill the palms of your hands. Leave blank, or paint with symbols and colors that invoke healing. Click together to clear energy.

Click your sticks, bones or stones together through your energy field, and anywhere in your home or office that needs energy shifted. Focus on your intention as you do so. And do as long as you feel is needed. Burn smudge before, during and/or after as you are guided to do.

Honor Spirit of the West as Your Ally

Call upon the Spirit of the West to assist you in honoring all you are, and all you have done, as well as to help you 'die' daily — to let go of what has been so you can be fully present to what is. Thank the West for helping you with the process of deepening within yourself so that you are able to be fully awake in the changes of life, fully present to the gifts given of all experiences, so they may flow easily through you.

Noya Rao - Mother Tree of Light
Katherine Skaggs © copyright 2019

*O*nce upon a time, long, long ago, the beautiful Divine Goddess of Creation Noya Rao came to Earth in a Bobansana crystal, when the Earth was barren of all life. With Noya Rao's power of creation, she gave birth to all the plants, creating a new world, full of life. As time passed, she decided to stay on Earth, becoming the most luminous tree, known as the Tree of Light.

A group of Shipibo peoples who live on the Amazon River in Peru, heard her story for many generations, but had never seen the wondrous tree. They believed Noya Rao had grown weary of the human condition and had left, causing the tree of light to become extinct. Then one night one of the shamans began to dream of her. He dreamed of a grove of five trees. He knew she was calling him to find her once again.

Yet, to find her, he knew it would be a treacherous adventure, for he would have to go into the jungle at night, without any light! This was a very perilous undertaking, as there are many dangerous creatures in the jungle that can kill you. Yet the shaman was determined to find her. So he and several other shamans left in the middle of the night, and headed to where he had seen her in his dreams.

The stories passed down through generations told the shamans that they would recognize Noya Rao in the darkness as her leaves are luminous when they fall to the ground! Sure enough, these shamans found her. Famed for her powers of creation, she is also known as a tree of wisdom, light and illumination. As an ally she is an excellent guide to Truth, moving one out of the darkness into the light.

Honor the Spirit of Death as Your Ally

Death is the great ally associated with the West who is here to help us let go. There are many names for the Spirit of Death, or spirit helpers associated with death. One of my favorites is Kali, a great goddess of death in the Hindu religion. She is the epitome of the Spirit of Death, as she is here to clean and clear away the energies born of ego that separate you from Spirit and create suffering. In her purest form, she is love and light, though she appears as a frightening black and blue female with wild hair, holding the decapitated head of a man. Her devotees revere her as a great protectress, helping one to align with the Divine, cleaning unconscious, lustful ways.

Are you afraid of death? Or do you embrace it as a powerful ally?

Do you welcome the end of cycles, the death of a job, death of a relationship, death of a loved one, and the always impending death of your own physical body? You are not alone if you are afraid of endings. The ego and false personality relentlessly convinces us that the known misery is better than the unknown, even when we are aware of great promise and possibility awaiting us.

Get to know Death as your ally, however, as it is one of the most important and powerful allies on the shamanic path. As you complete any cycle, any task, any relationship, it is most important that you do so in the best manner that you can, where you completely let go of the past experiences. Whether it be the stories and experiences of childhood, whether pleasant or difficult, or the energies of this last day, the West and Death are here to assist you in letting go, so you can be fully present for this moment. Death assists us in cutting the cords, dropping our attachments, and ultimately releasing all of the challenging patterns born of the past, and of old ways of being.

The Spirit of the West and the Spirit of Death teaches that it is more important how you finish things than how you start them. This is how we evolve!

Initiation and Shamanic Death

The greatest challenges we meet along the adventures of our earth walk are the soul initiations that have the potential of catapulting us into a new way of being. These are the experiences that cause us to stretch and grow, to go beyond comfort and ease, to temper our very beings into an expanded version of ourselves. I have experienced it over and over in my life. I have also observed it in others who have endeavored upon the shamanic path. All of the old, worn out ways of being and stories that hold us in suffering, arise and create discomfort. Everything that lacks harmony comes to our attention. Then, as we awaken our consciousness, we must change. We must clean away the gnarled patterns of fear, the old stubborn distortions that cause pain and dis-ease. We must undergo the shamanic initiations to shed the past, the shamanic death of the ego. With great courage, by doing so, we are blessed into greater harmony and joy. Initiation and shamanic death are unavoidable as you endeavor to grow, to change, to heal, and to awaken. These are essential aspects to complete restoration of the soul.

I have had several shamanic deaths along the way. One is enough, but more than one? Apparently, I had a lot of growth that I desired this time around!

My first shamanic death came into my path after a quite busy and successful cycle. During that time, I worked easily 60-80 hours a week. I loved every part of the experience, but often ignored what my body needed. I also ignored guidance I was getting for expansion, to change it up and to move into a different direction with my work. I ignored the whisperings in my head and heart, as I didn't know how to make the changes. As time passed everything got more difficult, and I began to manifest illness in my body. I was on overload but stubbornly would not step away from this life, as I didn't know how in that moment. I was in an initiation, but was consciously ignoring the signs to shift.

Well, the Spirit of Death came in and basically kicked my butt. The illness laid me down one day and I literally could not get up. I was very sick and unable to run my business, or anything else. Over a period of 18 months I crashed and burned completely. I lost my health, a relationship, my finances, and my business. After 7

1/2 years of great success, I found myself closing everything down in my business, so I could rest. I was forced to rest for a full year, unable to work. And when I did begin to work again, I was only able to work for 20 hours a week in a dead-end job that had nothing to do with my passions. I was now in survival mode. "Where the heck did my life go?" As I gained some strength I moved on to a better paying job in corporate America for another five years. Again, where did I go? Where did my life go? I often wondered how I got stuck in this loop that was only to make money to survive and get back on my feet again.

After what seemed like a very long time in my earth walk, I was finally given an opportunity to shift out of corporate American by creating a new business with a friend. I jumped at the opportunity. I left the uncomfortable corporate world of ordinary reality and leaped into a spiritually-focused business opportunity. Though all seemed well enough as we built this business, my business partner wanted out only three months after opening. This left me in a tenuous financial situation once again, where I could lose my finances and sense of security at the least!

This time, faced with imminent change and potential loss on many levels, I chose differently. There was no way I was going to lose everything again. And there was no way I was going back to a meaningless job just to make money. So, I diligently focused on what I wanted, rather than what I was losing. This time, instead, I used my gifts, focused on what I could do and how to be in service, and I moved into greater alignment yet again with my soul's path. Though it seemed things were falling apart once again, they were actually falling into place for my future here and now. As difficult as it was, this turned out the be the best thing in the world, far beyond what I could have imagined for myself.

I was in a complete reset, the Shamanic Death process, and an initiation into new life.

Symptoms of Initiation and Shamanic Death: Stagnation; unhappiness; stress experienced physically, mentally, emotionally, and spiritually; health issues; financial issues; feeling there must be another way but can't find it; the urge to move forward into a new way of life, but afraid to make changes. .

Be honest with yourself as you begin to recognize need for change, perhaps the sort of change that brings you to leave a job or a relationship, to go into therapy or into a life-changing shamanic program of deep transformation, or to change careers entirely. When you are fully honest with what makes you happy or unhappy, you can choose how to address the situation consciously, and with help. It is time to face your fears, and to courageously open to new ways of being. This always begins within.

Use the practices and tools within this book to first of all lovingly clean the Hucha and trauma that is connected to the stagnation. Do your best to move to a neutral and objective perspective with the practices given. Stop, rest, return to your breath, return to your heart. What if the most exciting adventure is about to birth into your life as you let go?

Sacrifice to Shift Out of the Shadow of the West

The word sacrifice literally means *to make sacred*. This is important to understand, as the West is the place of completion, release and death, brutally ending all that is finished, dead and done in your life. The West doesn't fool around, nor does it allow excuses to get in the way of death. It says, "DONE." Pay attention, so as to release with ease, staying in flow.

Clean your closets, on all levels from the physical closets to the recesses of your mind and emotions. Take time to do a give-away, where you let go and release items in your home. What needs to be gifted to someone else? What needs to be donated to a charity? When you take time to physically clean your world and let go, you will find a corresponding release happening within you both mentally and emotionally. This will also bring physical relaxation and peace.

Problems Sacrificing Create Suffering

If you find it difficult to let go, whether it be a physical item or an old story of how you 'been done wrong', there is a good chance you have an attachment to a time in the past that is causing suffering on some level, conscious or unconscious. Expectations and disappointments are part of the shadow patterns born of loss. These attitudes and their associated emotions contribute to any need you may have to hold on or control the outcome. All attachments are created from fear-based patterns. If you have a fear of losing something or someone, there is a fear pattern driving you to hold on. Use smudging, ceremony, and shamanic journey to release and to restore yourself. Work with the Spirit of West in all ways suggested to restore harmony.

The West is the Door to the Ancestors

As we move inward, we travel through the door of the West, opening a portal into the dreamtime and the ancestral realm. This gives us greater access to our ancestors and the world of Spirit.

Our ancestors are all who have walked before us. We particularly think of them as our parents, grandparents, and great grandparents, etc. Yet, the wisdom of the Lakota says to us, "*Mitakuye oyasin*" — "All are my relations." Tree, water, sky, earth, animals, brothers, sisters, and those that have taken their spirit walk are our kin. All is connected.

The Q'ero people of the Andes say "*Kausay pacha*" — "All is connected, an abundance of living energy." All is life and all has the essence of love. All are children of the Great Mother and Father — in spirit and physical form.

These ancestors who now are in the spirit world, once were in a physical body to experience love, sorry, joy, and the pain of being human. They have another perspective now that they are in the spirit world, and are able to support, provide guidance, teachings, healing, forgiveness, and even protection. Just because they are in the spirit realm doesn't mean they are more evolved than you, however. Some are, and some are not. There are ancestors who benefit and heal because you are doing your work, healing and awakening. They observe and respect your journey.

There are different types of ancestors you can call upon as well. You have specific familial ancestors, such as your grandparents, great grandparents, and lineage specific to this incarnation and its DNA heritage. They can be very helpful in healing specific ancestral patterns and are often offer much love and protection.

There are also ancestors specific to land areas, known as Land Ancestors. These territorial or land ancestors are stewards and spiritual guides connected to a specific piece of land, area, or territory.

You also have spiritual ancestral lineages, often who are very enlightened ancestors, such as Archangel Michael, Buddha, Christ, Kuan Yin, Mother Mary, White Buffalo Calf Woman, etc. These are ancestors that your soul has repeatedly chosen to work with. Have you ever felt an affinity to Buddhism, or Native American teachings, yet in this life you are from another culture and religion? Pay attention to these inclinations, as they most likely shed light on connections to your spiritual ancestral lineage. You may have had significant lifetimes in Egypt, or as a Buddhist monk and easily connect with the wisdom beings of that lineage. There are infinite possibilities and a particular ancestor could be in multiple categories.

Ancestral Patterns

Ancestral patterns can be patterns specific to your physical genetics, as well as patterns born of the cultural imprints left behind from earlier generations. They can also be the energetic imprints that you carry from other lives. The ancestral patterns passed down hold particular beliefs, gifts, talents, and even traumas that are passed on generationally.

Often times a family will have the pattern of a particular talent. Most everyone in the family is a musician, artist, scholar, doctors, and so on. You most likely chose this lineage to support your experience of that particular talent. And, what if you were the one who didn't get the musician or artist or doctor gene? Then I would say that you jumped into this ancestral patterning to be the different one, the one who had her own individuated path, the one who must stray from the norm to be happy. This opportunity is a lesson of courage, to be your own person, authentic and uniquely herself.

The patterns of our ancestors are passed down generation to generation. If there is love and harmony, this is passed on. If there is fear, fright and trauma, this is passed on.

Releasing Ancestral Patterns

When I began to experience more advanced shamanic work, I sat in sacred ceremony with the potent jungle plant medicine ayahuasca, whom I will refer to as Grandmother.

In my very first ceremony with Grandmother, I went deep within my soul's matrix, where I amazingly saw my father, at age 17, as a prisoner of war, captured and held by the Japanese during WWII. He experienced fright, shock, and trauma from being captured on Wake Island at the beginning of the war.

A young, thin, traumatized prisoner of war, who would one day be my father, stood before me. I sensed his suffering deep within my body and my soul. Tears streamed from my eyes, and I immediately understood why I had carried so much suffering in my own body and emotions this life. I began to pray the Hawaiian shamanic practice of forgiveness to release suffering and to restore balance. I released and released and released until there was nothing left to release. When completely emptied, the image and awareness of my father disappeared from in front of me.

Then, I sensed the energy of WWII, and the suffering of humanity for the heart-wrenching mistakes made to get into this war, for the incredible losses, and the hopelessness. Again, I began to weep and pray ho'oponopono, releasing, releasing and releasing, until there was nothing left to release. The energy didn't stop there. I found myself in a past Mayan lifetime of suffering. Again, weeping, I prayed ho'oponopono, releasing and releasing, until this too, disappeared.

Purged of these sufferings, I found myself in Egypt, in the presence of Isis and the energy of wisdom in the ancient goddess temples. As a priestess I sat in a place of deep meditation and love, surrounded by love and wisdom, sending this energy through time and space to restore balance in all who suffered.

Ancestral patterns offer many gifts and not just challenges. Having the opportunity to 'see, sense and experience' the suffering of my father, of humanity in WWII, as well as the Mayan and Egyptian energies gave me an understanding not only to what I wanted to release through these interfaces, but what gifts I brought to this dream. Through my ceremonial work, I was able to release the idea that I must have done something wrong to have chosen this family, where I felt I did not belong, and often experienced suffering. Instead I came to understand that I chose this ancestral lineage to bring love, compassion, and healing it, because I was capable of doing so. This choice was one of initiation, into holding and expressing greater light, love and compassion for my own self as well as others.

Your ancestors are always available and in service to your healing and awakening process. Take time with the practices given in this section, and throughout the book to learn to commune with your ancestors, so you may receive their love and support. Call upon them any time to assist you in releasing fear and trauma, focusing you back into the light and love of your true essence, and that true essence of every ancestor and soul in your lineage.

Recapitulation - The Toltec Way to Healing Ancestral Trauma and Fear

Recapitulation is an ancient Toltec technique to release misaligned energy, fear, trauma, and turmoil caused by our interactions with others. The use of recapitulation isn't a one-time shot, but a practice that requires attention throughout our lives… as often as possible!

The Toltec will tell you that every time you meet with another person that you exchange energy with one another. In the process, we imprint one another through our beliefs, our judgments, our praises, our emotional energies, and our physical actions. We have now added another dimension to this process of imprinting through social media, and digital technology, the constant streaming of news, and the endless supply of Twitter, Facebook, YouTube, etc. People's opinions, emotions, and thought forms constantly fly into our awareness. We don't have to be in physical contact to be deeply affected by this energy.

The more emotional the exchange, the greater the impact. The bigger the numbers of people expressing fear or love, the greater the effect. Currently, each of us is dealing with extensive fear patterns expressed through the discord of humanity. Whether it be social and economic dissonance, climate change, or other challenges, we are all feeling it the influences of this disharmony, igniting any fear we may carry. The effects of such challenging imprints and emotional exchanges, cause energy loss and take your systems out of balance, out of harmony, causing unhappiness, and possibly illness.

When we clear the psychic energies of others that have imprinted into our fields, we are more conscious of our own thoughts and feelings, uncluttered by the opinions, strong feelings, and attitudes others express. We can calm ourselves and view our own actions and attitudes more objectively through recapitulation. This helps us become more neutral to all situations, moving into the observer role. From this place we can choose more wisely and harmoniously, with less reaction to what we 'think' is going on in our world.

Use the practice of recapitulation to clear energy and to be in integrity with your own self. This will bring you a sense of freedom and centeredness in your true self.

The Practice of Recapitulation

In the true Toltec tradition of recapitulation, you are told to make a list of all the people you have ever met or interacted with since you were born for this practice. Insane, and a very long task indeed! How in the world could you ever remember all these folks? I am not sure, but I suppose this would be a practice that could be a life task.

To start, let's simplify and begin with a list of five people with whom you have conflict and where you need resolution. (Add to this list as desired as you clear away the old.)

~ Make a list of five people with whom you have and lack of harmony, conflict, or feel drained when you are around.

~ Write out the story of your challenge for each person onto their own sheet(s) of paper. Write out the specific interactions where you were drained, hurt, disempowered, angered and left without energy. Make this as long of a story as you want, from the memories that still haunt you. Commit the words, the feelings, the internal movie and dialogue of the situation onto paper. Make sure all the stories and interactions that keep you trapped in an old energy and old identity are addressed.

~ Go to your meditation room or altar, or a nice quiet place where you can move inward, preferable in a dark or dim room. Smudge and prepare your space for a sacred ceremonial process.

~ Call in your guides and helpers, particularly the Spirit of the West and Owl, to assist you in clearing these patterns.

~ Drop a grounding cord into Mother Earth and ask for her assistance.

~ Surround yourself in a bubble of pink light and unconditional love. Focus on the power of love and compassion to hold you in the highest frequencies possible as you clean away the Hucha of these imprints.

~ Choose the person and the story that you want to release and heal first from your list. Place a bubble of pink light around this person and all the stories of discord. Ask your angels and guides to come forth to assist each of you from the soul level to the human experience. Ask again that love dissolve the discord as you transmute the Hucha.

~ Visualize the person and the situation in as much detail as possible. The more details you have of your experience, the better it is in your process to let go. It is time to release every part of this conflict so it no longer has any power over you.

~ Now, turn your head all the way to your left shoulder. With your intention and all of your imagination, with a sweeping breath from left to right shoulder, breathe in all of your energy lost in this situation.

~ From your right shoulder, turn your head slowly to the left shoulder breathing out the imprinted energy of the person and situation of this challenging experience.

~ Repeat, breathing in your energy from the situation, and then breathing out the energy of the person and situation.

~ Repeat, repeat, repeat... go scene by scene until every memory of the experience and every grain of the imprinted energy is gone. Repeat, repeat, repeat, until you have also breathed in every breath of your soul's energy displaced in this past experience.

~ When you are complete, return completely to center with your breath, face forward, head up. You are home now. State out loud, "This is done. I am restored and renewed. All is well. So be it."

~ Then move on to the next memory and repeat the same process.

Once you have completed this practice, stop telling stories over and over that keep you in past fear, fright, and trauma. Practice living in this moment. Practice being in harmony, finding the blessings in life, and making change when life is out of harmony.

It is time to take your energy back, to reclaim your power, and to experience what it is like to be you. Try it.

Harvesting the Good

Thank You, Spirit of the West,
for Assisting Me in Harvesting the Good in My Life

The West reminds us that it is good to reflect upon our past experiences, whether it be at the end of the day, a week, a month, a season, a year, or a lifetime, and to gather up the blessings and harvest of each experience. This integrative process is very important if we are to become wise through the journey of the earth walk. Even when life is difficult, there is always a blessing to be found, if only you will look for it.

In alignment with the West, reflect at the end of the day, the end of a season, and the end of any cycle to harvest the good. Practice stillness and observation. Take time to digest what you have experienced, and you will find the blessings.

Here is an example of a West Prayer:

*H*ello, Spirit of the West. Thank you for being my ally of of good *endings, graduations, and death. Help me to release and let go with gratitude and grace. Help me to find the good and the valuable within all of my experiences. Then clean me of the tears, the grief, and the fears so I may completely let go of my experiences. Thank you for assisting me nourishing myself from every experience. Thank you for helping me to be present now. Thank you for the wisdom that comes in the process of this important cycle of life.*

West Altar Work

Give Your Hucha to Spirit of the West

~ Place everything you want to release onto the altar. Thank Spirit of the West and Great Spirit for taking these from you now.

~ Smudge yourself and your space.

~ Sit and be still. Focus inwardly and connect to your heart, and the Spirit of the West, and all your allies and ancestors through your intention, gratitude, and prayers.

~ Place everything you need to let go of onto the altar in the West (through intention, visualization, or written word.)

~ Now imagine that the sun is setting. As the sun sets over the horizon, imagine that the altar is being pulled into the setting sun. Imagine the Spirit of the West taking everything and composting it for you. Give gratitude to the West for its power and support.

~ Sit in the stillness, grounding down into Mother Earth. Breathe in peace and presence.

~ When complete, breathing from crown to toe, centering, then open your eyes restored and renewed.

~ Journal anything of importance about your experience. Acknowledge the work is done.

Polar Bear Shaman of the North
Katherine Skaggs © 2020

CHAPTER 10

SPIRIT OF THE NORTH

Nighttime • Winter

Rest • Regeneration

Wisdom • Home of the Elders

Dreaming • Place of Power

Observation • Right Timing

The North is the Seasonal Cycle of Winter

The North brings us into the barren stillness of Winter's cold, dark cycle. Mother Nature appears to die and become very still, at least in the Northern hemisphere. The leaves of the trees have vanished, the ground is cold, perhaps even covered in snow, and there is no apparent life. The North teaches us to go within, to the underground, beneath the surface of all that appears to be dead, into the world of darkness and that which is unknown. Here we can enter back into a place of rest, the dreamtime, the great void. It is time to can integrate, become wise and replenish.

The North is Also the Cycle of Nighttime

The Night also brings the medicine of the North same as Winter. The North is the space between endings of the West and beginnings of the East. In the night we enter dreamtime once again. This is an essential cycle of reset and preparation for your new day.

The North is the Place of Rest, Regeneration, Power

The North is the perfect place and cycle to rest, regenerate and be restored into our true power. Without this rest, your body will literally die! It is a must to stop, to let go of all the activities of the day, so your physical self, as well as your mental, emotional and spiritual self may be restored and replenished.

Reflection, Observation, Right Timing, and Right Action

When you move into the position of the North, and the power of stillness, the powers of reflection and observation begin to work magically within you and your life. This brings wisdom, as well as patience and the ability to know when to act, and when to be still. Effortlessness, grace, and ease come with these powers, along with the power of right timing.

As the wise one, the elder and the master of your experiences, you no longer have the impatience of the adolescent child who wants to grow up now. Have you ever been impatient and tried to hurry a situation, possibly forcing something to happen before it was ready? I think of the new farmer who goes out daily to see if his seeds are growing. One day he is so impatient, he digs up a row of seeds to see if anything is happening. Well, you know what happens next. They all die, because he didn't understand the power of nourishment and trust for the process, the cycle, and the season of these seeds.

Cultivate patience and trust as the power of the North moves you into reflection.

The Time of the North is That of Integration and Dreaming the Future

The North and its powers of stillness, reflection, and observation bring integration and wisdom. This a time for weaving the understandings of all that has been, bringing wisdom and peace. Surrounded by the quietness and stillness of the night and winter, be mindful, watchful, and observant of all within and without. Look for the synchronicities reflected in these weavings, as well as right relationship with all things and all cycles. The North returns us to the connectedness and oneness of all life, and to the flow of Creation.

Honor all that has come before. Nourish yourself with everything you have experienced. Reflect. Choose anew, based on this wisdom. Dream with greater clarity and power.

The Medicine of the North is Wisdom, Effortless Action, Synchronicity

When in the positive energies of the North, taking time to rest, play and regenerate is easy. You are balanced and in the flow between your waking, active state, and your inner, meditative, rest-filled state. You go to bed with ease, and sleep deeply, gaining much needed rest. You enjoy spa days, vacation time, meditation, and time for Self. You pay attention to your dreams, intuition, and inner voice. Life is both effortless and synchronistic.

The Shadow of the North is Struggle

Struggle, obligation, and never having enough time expresses the shadow energy of the North. The North calls upon you to stop and to go within.

If you find yourself in struggle, move back into the place of the West and address what you need to let go of so you can become still. What beliefs and fears tell keep you from stopping? What do you need to complete? What thoughts, projects and feelings get in the way of trusting that you can be still and move inward into the silence, into the void? Step into ceremony now, to clean and to clear the fear and the patterns that keep you in struggle. It is time to clear, smudge, take a vacation, do ceremony, or enjoy a long healing bath. Effortless action will come when you actually stop all the motions you are going through. If you feel you don't have time... hint, hint... this is the point! STOP! Have faith in the power of stopping and regrouping.

If the soil is tired and depleted, nothing will grow. It needs nutrients that will replenish its ability to nurture the seeds that are planted. It needs a rest from what it has done over and over again, perhaps not even growing any crops for a full season or two. It is time to compost the manure, the old patterns, the old stories, and allow a replenishment of nutrients that will make it ripe for planting in a season or two. Just as any field for growing crops needs rest and replenishment, you, too, need to replenish so you can grow your life with ease and fulfillment.

Earth is the Element of the North

The element of earth urges us to pay attention to Mother Earth's cycles, to listen to her wisdom, to her omens, and her guidance. She reminds us that all life are kin, and that we are all connected. Everything you do to yourself, you do to another. Everything you do the Earth, you do to yourself, and all your kin.

The Earth speaks loudly to humanity now, in this time of transformation, urging us to return to learn from our ways, and to return to balance, to respect all life. The waters, the lands, and the creatures all speak loudly, telling us that we are at an end of a way of being that is not sustainable. To become wise, to be healed and unified, we must change now and return to a place of harmony where we respect all life, all of the earth, all of the animals, all of the peoples. Only in this way will the species of the human tribe become whole again. Only will all our relations come to peace again.

The Totems of the North

Jaguar is a very powerful totem of the night time. Jaguar teaches about power, patience, right timing, observation and effortless action. Jaguars, and many big cats, have great patience in waiting in stillness of the night for just the right moment when their prey is within reach. They situate themselves at just the right place, such as a crossing where prey walks on their way to water. They sit without any effort at all, knowing that their prey will come soon enough. Then, at just the right moment, they pounce with great accuracy and success, using little energy and effort to achieve their goal. If you have been wasting your energy by staying busy, call upon Jaguar to assist you in sitting still and observing your world, so you might learn the power of patience and effortless action.

In the Northern Hemisphere, Bear is a well-known totem of the North, and the time of Winter. Bear has a full belly as she enters the cave to hibernate for her deep Winter's sleep. Here she enters into a place of deep regeneration that takes her into dreamtime, where she dreams anew of her adventures when she awakes to frolic in the time of Spring.

Many Native American traditions turn to the Buffalo as their totem of the North. Buffalo teaches us that all beings on earth are our kin, to be grateful for all that is given, and to respect all life. Buffalo reminds us to respect Mother Earth, respect all people no matter how different, respect the elders, the wise ones and the way showers. Respect yourself by giving of what you have. Buffalo shows us what respect is as it gives its life and all it is made up to provide for others. In doing so it respects itself and those it serves. With Buffalo comes the wisdom of White Buffalo Calf Woman, who teaches us that all life is sacred.

The Instrument and Sounds of the North

The rattle is an excellent instrument for cleaning and clearing hucha and trauma, breaking away the distorted patterns, which you would think would make it an instrument of the West. However, it is considered the instrument of the North for its abilities to call home all parts of the soul that have been lost during their experiences around the Wheel of Life. You see, when the soul is on the grand adventure of being human, it often faces experiences that are laced with fear or fright, and, at times, trauma. If for any reason that fright and trauma were not cleaned away immediately after the experience, a piece of the soul is lost or fragmented, unable to return until there has been a clearing of that pattern.

When we live with trauma, fright, fear, PTSD, we are not whole in ourselves. We aren't quite right. In this manner we literally feel lost, often depressed, anxious, ungrounded, and completely out of sorts which can manifest mentally, emotionally, and physically. It is impossible to be in harmony when there is soul loss.

That is when the rattle comes in as an excellent instrument to both clear and to call home the soul parts so they can return. Harmony and balanced are restored in the process.

Call in Lost Soul Parts with Your Rattle

As with any ritual or practice, set a sacred space and container. You can do this exercise at your altar, in nature, or any place where you are safe and can create ceremony.

~ Light a candle, burn some sage, set your altar, and say your prayers.

~ Open the directions and call in all your allies and helpers. Call in the Spirit of the North and the spirit of your rattle to go to work for you. Call any other special allies who are really good at helping. I always call my owl and jaguar allies in this situation, as they are experts at gathering up any lost energy and soul parts.

~ Thank your rattle and bless it for the work it is about to do. Smoke it with white sage, palo santo, or sacred tobacco to prepare it for its work. Also make sure to smoke yourself.

~ If you have any particular situations that have caused fright, fear or trauma, ask your rattle and your allies to assist you in clearing those situations, one by one, or all at once, as you are guided.

~ Now, rattle through your energy field, in all the places where you feel constricted. Rattle with your focus on releasing each experience, blessing it as it leaves, so you can receive the energy and wisdom from the experience.

~ Rattle until you feel a shift or know something has left.

~ Once you have cleared the disharmonious energies, stop for a moment. Be still.

~ Clear your rattle, as well as yourself, with smoke once again before the next part.

~ Now focus on calling home all energy and soul parts that were lost in time and space during any traumatic or fear-filled experience, emotional exchange, or accident.

~ With intention, call home all lost energy and soul parts. Imagine with every shake of the rattle, energy returns home to you.

~ Rattle until you feel complete.

~ Then, put your rattle down, put both hands on your heart, and say, "I am here now. I am home now. I am complete." Feel yourself at home once again.

~ Then rest, absorb, soak in this energy. Allow yourself time to integrate, to reflect, and to be in your heart.

~ When you are done with your session, burn sweet grass to return the sweetness to life. Smoke your altar, your rattle, and most of all your own energy and physical being, to reset the blessings and sweetness into your life.

Honor the Spirit of the North as Your Ally

As you get to know the Spirit of the North and work with its energies, from the earnestness of your heart, ask the North to help you to receive, to stop doing, to rest, to take time for yourself, to trust, and to fill your reservoirs. Thank the Spirit of the North for providing this place of stillness, that you may truly respect yourself and all you have created.

Ask the Spirit of the North to give you guidance from the council fires of the ancestors who have walked this path before you, that you might honor and know their wisdom, too! Ask Spirit of the North to teach you stillness, humility, and silence, that you might listen well.

You can also call upon the Spirit of the North for getting a good night's rest, full of dreams for a new day. If you don't recall your dreams, call upon the North to take you on a dream journey.

Rest, Regeneration

Thank, You Spirit of the North,
for Assisting Me in Going Within

What is the quality of your sleep? Do you take time to be still, to walk in nature, to meditate, or vacation? Are there projects you have been working on and working on and working on that you need to give over to Spirit?

Before bedtime, take time to write your prayers to the Spirit of the North for supporting you in resting and regenerating yourself and areas of your life. Be honest. What is tired or worn out in you or your life? What do you need to do differently to rest and reset yourself?

- ~ Ask the Spirit of the North to assist you in relinquishing your hold on the outer world, so you may go within to the place of deep dreams and restoration. From this still place, you have the power to dream your outer world with greater clarity, power and harmony.
- ~ If you are not sure about any of the answers to your questions and requests, leave them blank. Take the paper and put under your pillow before you go to bed at night or into shamanic journey with Bear.
- ~ Smudge your bed and bedroom space.
- ~ Darken your room and call in the Spirit of Bear to take you into the cave of 'within,' so you may go deep into dreamtime.
- ~ Sit, or lie, and be still.
- ~ Focus inwardly and connect to your heart.
- ~ Use your breath or shamanic drum music to release your attention on your outer world, and begin to move inward to a restful journey space.
- ~ Journey or sleep until you are guided to awaken.
- ~ Record any dreams and awareness you receive in your journal.
- ~ What has Bear shown you? Do you have the answers to your questions? Continue this practice each night and you will come to the place of wisdom as you go deeper within each time.

Here is an example of a North Prayer:

Hello, Spirit of the North. I call you now before I sleep, to assist me in rest and restoration. Please come with your powers of dreamtime, to take me deep into the inner worlds of Spirit, that I may dream again, a new beginning for when I awake. Help me to integrate my experiences, that I am wise and restored at the deepest levels. Thank you for returning me to my power. Thank you for the answers I need to easily learn and grow.

Power and Empowerment

Thank You, Spirit of the North and Jaguar for Assisting Me in Taking Back My Power

~ Set your focus and intention to journey with the Spirit of Jaguar and the Night Medicine of the North.

~ Smudge your space and prepare it for going within.

~ Sit and be still.

~ Focus inwardly and connect to your heart. Gratefully invite in the Spirit of the North and Black Jaguar to support you in effortless action, acting in right timing with your dreams.

~ Ask Jaguar and the North to teach you to trust.

~ In the stillness and reflection, focus on any ripe opportunities in your life, such as buying a new house, changing jobs, or making some change.

~ Observe the motion and patterns of these experiences and dreams. Just as a Jaguar sits in the jungle and waits for her prey to walk by, you are being asked to be absolutely still to gaze upon your life circumstances.

~ What is ripe to act? What needs your patience?

~ Breathe. Pick the fruit only when it is ripe. Otherwise, leave it to another day. Then you will receive blessings and bounty.

~ When complete, journal your guidance and experience.

~ Take note of any actions you need to take to follow through on an opportunity.

~ Also take note of places in your life that you need to let rest, to let time show you the next step.

~ Then sit with each situation and bless it as it is now.

There is nothing to do except to accept it as it is, and to bless it. From a position of observation, you will know when to act, when to remain still, what to do or not do. If it is yours, it will come to you in clarity with ease.

There is no effort in this position, only acceptance and observation. Reserve your energy and you will know what you need to know when you need to know it. Then and only then will you need energy to act, as all in perfect timing.

North Altar Work

Rest, Regeneration, Reflection and Wisdom

Moving into the place of rest and regeneration is the natural state of winter and nighttime, and the medicine of the North. It is effortless and gives us the place to go within that we might explore dreamtime again. It is the place of reset and effortless, offering more power than we know.

~ Place objects symbolizing night, winter, bear, jaguar, buffalo and regeneration onto your northern quadrant of your altar.

~ Along with the sacred items and objects, place your prayers and intentions for regeneration and wisdom as you desire.

~ Smudge your altar and all the new items you have added to the altar.

~ Thank the Spirit of the North, as well as the allies symbolized by your power items for the ways in which they serve you.

~ Invoke the medicine of the North for good sleep, good reset, and good dreams to come.

~ Sit in silence and go within.

~ Rattle or play the sound of the rattle to call home all of self into present time.

~ Absorb this energy as you rest. There is nothing to do. It is time to receive.

~ Ground into Mother Earth. Breathe back to your body.

~ Go to bed!

Soul Essence Ra
Katherine Skaggs © 2020

CHAPTER 11

SPIRIT OF ABOVE — FATHER SKY

Divine Masculine

Light • Vision • Higher Perspective

Messages • Protection• Leadership

Divine Law • Heavenly Realm

Father Sky is Higher Vision and the Power of the Divine Masculine The power and medicine of Father Sky bring the guidance of the heavenly, higher vibrational perspective. Both gentle and strong, this Divine Masculine wisdom always lights the path with truth and unconditional love. Divine Law is the guide for living a harmonious and sacred life in the right relationship to all.

Father Sky, also Known as Above, Represents the Heavenly Realms and Inner Dimensions

Look up! Look within. Father Sky is the higher dimensional energy of the heavenly realms and higher states of consciousness. Above and within are interchangeable concepts. The heavenly realms may also be referred to as the inner dimensions of one's soul. Imagine going within to explore the deep inner regions of Spirit, of soul, as you would imagine flying to the outer reaches of the cosmos. Both can be explored simultaneously.

Father Sky is the Light

Father Sky is the light of the Central Sun and the light of the Divine Masculine. It is the activating light principle to 'awaken' and 'illuminate' our very consciousness, as the child of the Creator. Within our very beings is this same light, wanting to expand and to express.

Father Sky is the Place of Inspiration and Sudden Awareness/Awakening

Be open to the solar power of pure, spiritual light illuminating your thoughts, your visions, your feelings, your DNA. Inspiration comes from this higher awareness, bringing creativity and vision. In an instant, a sudden and unexpected insight can illuminate your life. In an instant, you can be awakened and healed when you connect to this powerful energy.

The Medicine of Father Sky is Authority, Vision, and Trust

The medicine of Father Sky and the heavenly realms guides directs, inspires, and brings complete trust that life is well, and all is in Divine order. You are held in wisdom and trust in the process of Divine law. When aligned with this medicine, you trust your vision, your knowing, your voice, and your choices. You are humble and lead by your illumined heart.

The Shadow of Father Sky is False Authority, Arrogance, Dominance, and Control

If you are feeling the need to control your life, to dominate others, to act in arrogance, or if you harbor a fear of being dominated, you are living in the shadows far from the light of Father Sky.

Stop giving your authority and power to others, particularly parents, teachers, and leaders that you either admire or fear. Know what truth is, and honor that in yourself as well as others when they express it. Then, take ownership of your own truth. Humbly, yet powerfully, speak and act in order with Divine Law; trust your wisdom and shine your light as a leader yourself. Be empowered alongside others. There is enough light to shine for all.

Overcoming Arrogance
Moving into the Light of True Authority and Leadership

To overcome arrogance and return to your true authority, you must address all ways you gave your power and knowledge over to that of another person or organization. To heal, take time to address abusive words, beliefs, and actions you experienced from an authority figure or organization of authority (such as your government, your church, or school) in any form. Face and admit these imprints, judgments, and beliefs that created suffering on any level, spiritually, mentally, emotionally, and physically. Then proceed to ceremony and ritual to clear them.

Use the tools you have been given so far to become honest. Clean your mind, your heart, your emotions, your physical self, and your spirit of all Hucha, of all envy, of all smallness, of all separation, all judgment. Work with your allies and Great Spirit to restore trust in your higher knowing.

Totems and Symbols of Father Sky

The many gods of mythologies around the world can each be looked upon as aspects and representations of Father Sky from different traditions such as Zeus, Jesus, Odin, Helios, Apollo, Ra, Horus, Wakea, Tateware, Thunder God, and many others.

The Sun is the main symbol of Father Sky. The elements of thunder, rain, and lightning represent additional heavenly powers from Above.

Eagle Totem
Katherine Skaggs © 2017

Birds are also seen as the totems of Father Sky. Eagle, hawk, and thunderbirds are often used to represent the power and vision of the Sky Father. Clouds, thunderbolts, lightning, and rain also symbolize the powers of the heavens. I also consider angels as messengers and helpers for the Sky Father.

Instruments and Sounds of Father Sky

Flute and wind instruments, as well as string instruments, can bring the heavenly sounds of the Sky Father to your heart and soul. To invoke the energy and assistance of Father Sky, consider playing recordings of music using these instruments or even play these musical instruments yourself.

Honor Father Sky as Your Ally

Father Sky personifies true leadership and justice. This justice is not based on man's laws and judgments but on the sacred, Divine Law of the Universe.

> Sacred law transcends man's law and is here to remind you that no man can keep you from what is divinely yours, that your heavenly gifts will manifest at exactly the right time.

Call upon Father Sky to guide you and help you receive the blessings of wisdom, grace, and perfect alignment with Divine Law. Thank Father Sky for the power of light and illumination, the power of the highest knowledge, the power of vision. Thank Father Sky also for the benevolence and blessings he shines upon you.

When honoring Father Sky, extend your gratitude and prayers to all of the heavenly realms. This may include angels, ascended masters, the star nation, and all higher consciousness beings from the higher dimensions. Many light beings come through the portal of the heavenly realms to assist us. The more you put your attention and gratitude upon the higher dimensions, the more aware you will become of their love and guidance.

As Above, So Below —
A Reflection of Father Sky and Divine Law

This Universal Law of As Above, So Below says that which is Below corresponds to that which is Above, and vice-versa, as well as 'so within, so without.' Whatever happens on one level of reality happens on all levels of reality — physical, emotional, mental, and spiritual. Do your best to understand and align with Divine Law when you recognize are out of balance. Call up your heavenly support system and Father Sky to assist you. Then look for the magic!

Karma —
The Law of Cause and Effect

Karma is not tit for tat, but the Universal Law of Cause and Effect. It is the recognition that there is cause and effect for every action. It is definitely related to the power of As Above, So Below. Call upon Father Sky to assist you in right view, right resolve, right speech, right conduct, right livelihood, right effort, right mindfulness, and right union/right action. This is also the wisdom of the shamanic Eightfold Path of Buddhism.

Journey with Father Sky
to Claim Your Light and Power

~ Set your journey space at your altar or outside in nature where you are safe and can go within.

~ Sit upon the great Earth Mother, feeling your body connecting to her energy and essence. Feel into how she holds you. Anchor into the present time.

~ Drop a grounding cord deeply to her core, ask her to hold you, feed you, and take your Hucha. Then draw her healing energy up through your grounding cord, up through your spinal column, up and out your crown, into a silver cord of light ascending into the heavens, connecting to the light above and the energy of Father Sky.

~ Feel/sense the energy return in a vast expanse of energy from Above to Below, showering your physical and energy bodies with pure light and Sami.

~ Breathe it in. Feel this flow through you, penetrating all the way back down to the core of Mother Earth.

~ As you breathe, feel the circulation from below to above, and from above to below. Allow your breath to circulate above to below, below to above, in a natural flow and rhythm of endless connection.

- Allow your breath to deepen your inner state of awareness. Then call one of your allies to assist you in flight into the heavenly realms and the consciousness of Father Sky.
- Take flight on the back of a bird, an insect, or an angel (or another being of Divine light), or in any other way Spirit and your guides would like to assist you.
- As are freed into the higher light and the realm of Father Sky, ask to be taken to the place of love and wisdom of Father Sky. Invite this light to awaken your inner light and power, your own knowing.
- If you have had any issues with authority within and around you, ask for the healing energies of Father Sky to embrace you, to illuminate and clear any misunderstandings or trauma that you have carried until now.
- Relax deeper and deeper with your breath and with the flight to Father Sky. Ask for any healing and guidance that you need most now.
- Stay within the journey as long as you like. When you feel complete, return to your body, breathing from crown to toe, still connected to both above and below, grounded both down and up.
- Sit and breathe, feeling yourself return with an expanded version of yourself, full of light and new understandings.
- Take time to journal what you need to record. Speak or write your prayers of gratitude. Acknowledge what you have experienced, putting both hands over your heart to anchor this energy.
- Drink some water or calming tea, and complete your ceremony by thanking Father Sky and all your helpers who came to support you in your journey.

◊Daily Notes to Self:

Prayers and Reflections with Father Sky

Prayers with Father Sky

Say hello to Father Sky at your altar, on a nature walk, in a sacred ceremony. Turn your head and your heart upwards, as well as inwards, to connect to Father Sky and the power of light. Recognize the power of this great energy that gives life to all. Be grateful and connect upwards. Visualize your connection to a great light in the sky, in the cosmos, shining down upon you, into your heart, your body, your mind, and your soul. Imagine the light penetrating deep into your physical and spiritual DNA. Be still and bathe in the light. Open to receive. Rest in this light. Rest in this wisdom and love, allowing it to animate you in time through inspiration and fullness.

Here is an example of a Father Sky Prayer:

Hello Father Sky. Thank you so much for your heavenly light, protection, and guidance. I call upon you now to bring more light into my heart, into my mind, into my body, and into my spirit. I ask that I become completely aware of your blessings in all of my life. I open to receive this energy that I may continue to fully awaken my own light body. Thank you for the blessings from above for all. May all my kin receive your blessings in their fullness.

Absorbing Sami from the Light — Charge Up with Father Sky

~ Sit outside into the morning light of the sunrise, at mid-day in the fullness of the Sun, or at the time of sunset.

~ Find a spot where you are comfortable and feel safe, where you can connect in your own sacred way with the energies of the Sun.

~ Turn the front of your body to the sun.

~ Turn your head upwards, with eyes closed or in a soft gaze to the sun.

~ Open your arms outward with palms open and up to receive the sun's warmth and light directly into your palms.

~ Inwardly say "hello" to the sun and Father Sky. Through your intention and focus, ask for this light to penetrate your body, energy bodies, and soul essence to charge you with light.

~ Breathe the light in through your mouth with your focus and intention. Imagine this light and warmth penetrating every part of you.

~ Allow the warm energy of the light (through your breath) to drop down your throat, past your thyroid, digestive tract, heart and lungs, and upper belly into your lower belly, settling down into your belly button region.

~ When you feel full of light and energy at this area, breathe in again and imagine this light overflowing downwards into your root and downwards to your feet until you are filled with light from crown to toe.

~ On the next breath in, overflow the light from your physical body into the auric egg of light surrounding your physical body. Do this until you become shiny and glowing all around and within.

~ Repeat nine times.

~ Seal the energy in by placing your hands over your belly button area. Hold to the count of 10, or as long as you feel the need to hold.

- Women - place your right hand on the belly button area, and cover with your left hand.
- Men - place your left hand on the belly button area, and cover with your right hand.

~ Relax your hands. Breathe three deep belly breaths, once again, drawing the energy from crown to toe, coming completely back into your body, and present time awareness.

Try this exercise in the early morning light of sunrise, in the mid-day sun, and at the setting sun. You may also try this at night time, connecting to the starlight and the moonlight.

Each offers a different, empowering light for charging your energy, as well as becoming connected to the various aspects of Father Sky's light and illumination powers.

Father Sky Altar Work — Connecting to the Light

Continue your altar work with your focus now on the benevolent power of Father Sky. Place feathers, candles, sacred objects, or images of lightning, clouds, sun, moon, and stars to represent Father Sky. Place flowers on the altar to attract the medicine of Father Sky and the Heavenly beings to your prayer space. Align your prayers through gratitude for the powers of light, illumination, and wisdom to assist and bless you and others.

Mama Gaia
Katherine Skaggs © 2006

CHAPTER 12

SPIRIT OF BELOW — MOTHER EARTH

Divine Mother • Mother Gaia • Pachamama
Sachamama • Compassion • Nurturing
Nature • Creation and Sacred Destruction
Motherhood • Fertility • Cycles
Birth/Death • Mother of All • Kinship

Mother Earth is the Divine Mother of Creation, Fertility, Birth, Motherhood, Blossoming, Cycles, Death, Sacrifice

Mother Earth and the medicine of below is the world of Spirit that has manifested into physical form. The Great Mother births that which has been in heaven. She is the Sacred Feminine womb of Creation, holding the seeds of possibility in her sacred womb container. She is the powerful Mother who gives birth to these seeds, giving them form and a place to grow. She is the elemental power of Mother Nature and all her cycles, from birth to death. She embodies the powers of possibility, birth, growth, sacred destruction, death, and renewal.

Mother Earth, Pachamama, and Mama Gaia are some of her many names. She is the ancestral Great Mother of all beings. She teaches us about the interdependence, kinship, and connectivity of all life.

Mother Earth gives us all we need, from our food to our waters to our shelters. She also teaches us the importance of respect and reverence that we may live in harmony with all life—the actions of one affect everyone and the whole.

Mother Earth is Associated with the Magic and Spirit of Life

We stand upon our Mother. She is our mesa, our sacred table, and our home. She gives us our bodies to experience with. She gives us the sacred waters and foods that fuel our bodies. She gives us the one-legged (trees, plants, streams, waters, mountains), the two-legged (humans and those who walk upright), the four-legged (the animals), the stone people, and the winged ones; our kin. She is the essence of magic and Spirit in all life.

Mother Earth is the Manifestation of Light into Form

If Father Sky is the Light, then Mother Earth is the animation of the Light into form. She is our place of experience. She shows us how our thoughts and beliefs, our emotions, and our actions create and manifest into the world of experience and form.

The Medicine of Below and Mother Earth is Harmony, Abundance, Gifts of Connection

From birth to adolescence to old age and death, from Spring to Summer to Autumn to Winter, Mother Earth teaches us all about possibility, birth, abundance, flow, harmony, and connection through all life. She is eternal life, harmonized by eternal movement.

Learning to walk with the powerful medicine of our Great Mother is to recognize and respect our connection to all life, to all our kin, to all our relations. This is the power to walk in harmony with others, no matter your differences. Embodying this medicine helps you recognize each person, each animal, each plant, and every expression of Mother Earth as an ally and part of your tribe.

This medicine teaches us that no one is separate from ourselves. All Earth beings have medicine they offer. The Plant and Tree people teach us to send our roots deep into Mother Earth for grounding. They give us food, healing medicines, and other gifts for making our clothing, tools, and homes. The Water People share their understanding of flow through our feelings and emotions. The various Four-Legged clans bring diverse teachings and gifts about being in a body and living on the Earth. The Winged Ones teach us how to take flight, to lighten up, and to rise above so we may see with greater clarity and wisdom.

The heartbeat of Mother Earth has a song and a rhythm that lives in each of us, guiding us, directing us. Her heartbeat gives direction to our own spiritual GPS. Aligning with the medicine of Mother Earth brings harmony by walking in beauty with respect for all life.

The Shadow of Mother Earth is Lack, Fear, and Being Out of Balance

When in the shadows with Mama Gaia, we fall out of balance, unaware of the cycles and symbols of life right before us. We are off-key in the greatest symphony ever formed. We miss the beauty and the gifts right in front of us. We are unable or unwilling to receive the abundance of what is given, disrespecting the blessings and sacredness of resources given. Fear ensues, and we fear the vast depth and breadth of the Great Mother and all her kin.

Humankind is currently way out of balance, struggling with the fallout of many generations of imbalance — expressed as greed, lack, the dominance of one over another, injustices and disrespect of one another, fear of one another, etc. Great trauma has occurred time and again of one people against another people, of one brother against another, in many generations to be named, all in the name of one group conquering another. The imbalances have continued all around us as we have been asleep in our consciousness. Humankind has poisoned not only one another but the entirety of our environment for generations, to our waters, our air, our soil, our food, and all creatures that live upon our planet. All of the whole has suffered through the unconscious and selfish actions of many.

When we as a species turn against our fellow human and all the creatures around us, and the earth itself, we have turned against our own selves. Mother Earth teaches us through our experiences that 'what we do to another, we do to ourselves.' You cannot harm another without harming yourself.

In the shadow medicines of Mother Earth, every inhabitant is called to a time of reckoning for this planet and the species of humankind. This is a cycle of endings. Lack of respect for all life has created an imbalance that is not sustainable on any level. The greater the fear, the greater the imbalance. Mother Earth will persevere through the imbalance, but humans cannot if they do not take responsibility and purify their ways.

To come into balance and heal, we must take personal responsibility for our lives and how we live them. Are you in harmony with your environment? Are you in harmony with other humans? Are you in harmony with the animal and plant life? What habits need purification so you can live in peace within and with the world around you?

It is time to choose now, to honor the beauty of Mother Earth, and to honor the beauty within your own being. Then you can honor others and all creation on this planet. Practice good boundaries in alignment with harmonious values for self and others. Clean your heart of anger and judgment. Be fierce for good, for self, and for all creatures. Imagine this for others, and encourage it through your own tenacity and benevolence. Remember, as you do unto others, you do unto yourself. This is the only path for your own soul's evolution.

With every breath you take and heart-centered action you express, you are the change that influences the destiny of Mother Earth and humanity. This is the power we each have to heal the imbalances and to once again walk in balance and beauty upon our great Mother.

Earth is the Element of Mother Earth

The elemental energy of Mother Earth is that of the earth itself, of course. Connect to this Great Mother Earth by honoring her cycles and all of her creations as your kin. Give offerings to the land in gratitude for all she gives. Sit upon her in reverence, walk upon her softly in the presence of her power, soaking in her energy and generous nature. Practice walking upon her with respect and in observation of her beauty.

Totems and Symbols of Mother Earth

Mama Gaia, Pachamama, and Mother Earth are names symbolizing the energies of the Great Earth Mother. Totems and images are born in each culture worldwide to embody the power and energy of this Divine Mother.

A bowl of soil from a sacred site symbolizes the power of the Earth Mother's womb and potential for manifesting dreams into form; a bowl of water from a sacred well, stream, or ocean symbolizes her flow and power of purification; a candle represents the element of fire and the light of heaven on earth; a feather represents the power of air and the messages from above. All express the creative life force and potent energy Mother Earth offers for bringing harmony.

All creatures, whether 2-legged, 4-legged, or winged, symbolize the various powers and gifts of this earth. Buffalo is a powerful symbol of the Earth Mother, representing respect and abundance. All is given for us to live well.

The totem of Deer is another powerful Mother Earth symbol of sacrifice, gentleness, and unconditional love. Deer is revered for fertility, motherhood, regeneration, and the rebirth of the sun (winter solstice symbols).

Honoring Mother Earth as Your Ally

Call upon Mother Earth, offering deep gratitude that all is given. Recognize and express appreciation for all the gifts she brings you, whether it be the food on your table, or the clothes on your back and the home you live in. She is the provider. Thank her for all she gives, and then give a blessing or offering back to her. Give her offerings of your heart, your words, your song, and items that feed her.

This practice of reciprocity brings an exchange of energy and is foundational in all shamanic practices. I find this is especially tangible when working with Mother Earth. As we practice focusing our energy and attention in gratitude with this Mother Earth, we can see the energy return easily, from the beauty of Spring to the baroness of Winter. Mother Earth will teach you and return blessings to you constantly if you are walking in awareness of her.

White Buffalo Calf Woman
Katherine Skaggs © 2007

The Teachings of White Buffalo Calf Woman

A Love Story of Living a Sacred Life in Harmony with Mother Earth

*M*any moons ago, there was a great famine on the earth. As a result, a wise Lakota Chief sent two braves out to hunt for food. While looking across the plains, the young men saw a large white cloud in the distance, traveling their direction. As it came closer, the braves saw a beautiful woman dressed in white buffalo skins, emerging from the cloud.

One of the young braves lusted for her, and, turning to the other brave, said he would have his way with her and make her his wife. The other brave knew she was sacred and told him no, that he must respect her for she was Divine. The first brave ignored his friend and began to pursue the beautiful woman.

White Buffalo Calf Woman, being Divine, was omniscient and aware of the braves' thoughts. So she beckoned him into her open arms and enfolded him in her robe. As the first brave moved into her embrace, a white cloud enfolded the couple. The other brave watched in horror as his friend moved from young to old until he fell into a pile of dust.

The remaining brave pulled his bow and arrow out, and aiming it at the woman, asked who she was.

The holy woman beckoned him forward, telling him that no harm would come as she could see the purity in his heart. She told him to go to his people and to have them prepare for her to come, for she would teach them about living a sacred life, about restoring their health, and about well-being.

She proceeded to his village to teach his people seven sacred rites of purification, returning them to living life as a sacred ceremony. Among these rites, she taught them about using the sacred ceremonial pipe for sending their prayers to Spirit, as well as the purification rite of Sweat Lodge.

◊ Daily Notes to Self:

Prayers and Reflections with Mother Earth

Praying and Connecting with Mother Earth

Go outside into nature. Take time to connect to her, feeling her under your feet and all around you. Bring her offerings of flowers, fruits, cornmeal, and sacred tobacco in gratitude and reciprocity. Honor her visible and invisible powers by feeding her. Bless her! Be still and present to all she gives. Then you will experience her many signs, symbols, and messages.

Here is an example of a Mother Earth Prayer:

Hello, dear Mother Earth, Mother of my body and all of this world, Mother of all life. Thank you for your powers of birth, life, death, composting and birth again. Thank you for teaching me about the ever flowing of cycles. Thank you for all my kin here, the animals, the birds, the plants, the land, the waters, and all of life. May I live in greater harmony and blessings with all life.

Grounding Tree of Life Meditation
with the Great Mother Gaia

~ Sit upon Mama Gaia. Feel your bottom upon her soil.

~ Imagine you are like a tree, dropping a tap root all the way down into her fertileness, visualizing it sinking all the way into her center. Imagine it making a sound when it reaches her core.

~ As always, say, "Hello!" and "Thank you!"

~ Through your tap root, imagine two channels of energy.

- One channel is for releasing Hucha, just as you would drop compost remains into a garden, and your carbon dioxide waste from your breath into the environment for the plants and trees. With this exchange channel, you release what no longer serves you, and Mother Earth feeds on it!

- Imagine the other channel drinks the life force of Mother Earth into your body and energy bodies, filling you with Sami.

~ Draw the energy of the Mother up your root, into and up your spinal column, feeding your energy centers, your organs, your bones, your blood, and very DNA, moving upwards to the top of your crown.

~ Once you are filled up with this Sami, imagine the energy channel becomes a silver cord moving out of your crown, extending all the way to the heavens, grounding upwards into Father Sky.

~ Once you have connected with this light from Above, imagine in a continuous flow, the energy returns through your aura and down your root system from crown to toe, from heaven to Earth.

~ In gratitude, bless the Earth Mother and the Sky Father, blessing yourself and the world around you as you bathe in this high-frequency light, love, and life-giving force.

Mother Earth Altar Work
Connecting to the Web of Life and Creation

Go outside into nature. Take time to connect to her, feeling her under your feet and all around you. Bring her offerings of flowers, fruits, cornmeal, and sacred tobacco in gratitude and reciprocity. Honor her visible and invisible powers by feeding her. Bless her! Be still and present to all she gives.

Guardians
Katherine Skaggs © 1995

CHAPTER 13

GREAT SPIRIT

Creator • Great Mystery

Wakan Tanka • Source

Supreme Being • Universal Spiritual Force

Unity • Consciousness

Great Spirit is known by many names among various Native American peoples, such as Wakan Tanka, Great Mystery, One Who Has Made Everything, Maker of All Things Above, even Old Man Coyote. Regardless of what tribe or culture, Great Spirit is the ultimate representation of Universal Consciousness and Spiritual Creative Force. This Supreme Force is neither male nor female, though most often is personified as a male deity. Rather, Great Spirit is the wholeness of all Creation embodying both, and neither at the same time.

Great Spirit is in Everything

Imagine that Great Spirit gave birth to all form: the heavens, the galaxies, the earth, the directions, the elements, the humans, the animals, the waters, the mountains, the sky… everything and all the dimensions of experience. In doing so, the Great Spirit's essence, light, and consciousness imprinted into the DNA of all form, of all souls, of all existence. We are all the children of Great Spirit. You are the child of Great Spirit. Your heritage is to awaken the vast, creative intelligence within your very cells, both physically and spiritually.

Your DNA is 90% Spiritual, 10% Physical

Now, imagine this… your DNA isn't all physical! It is 90% spiritual and only 10% physical. With that being said, just imagine that the powerful gifts of the Creator are within you and are accessible as you go deeper upon your spiritual path. You are a Divine being of light. Look within yourself and all experiences in your life, and you will come to know this.

Great Spirit Animates Everything

Great Spirit IS the invisible life force and creative intelligence that animates all life. Great Spirit transcends time, space, direction, and location. Great Spirit lives within all creation and is eternal.

The Medicine of Creativity and Higher Consciousness

Great Spirit is pure creative life force and higher consciousness. Universal Laws and Truth express how this creative force works and gives us a guideline and playbook for living life in alignment and harmony with all of Creation. When living in harmony with spiritual law, we find ourselves happy, joyful, abundant, and at peace. We have great trust and truly know that all is well. We know who we are and can live completely in the moment as the creator and dreamer of our life.

The Shadow Medicine of Great Spirit is Being Lost, Empty, Unfulfilled

When you have lost your connection to Great Spirit, you have lost your way in the earth walk. You have no trust or faith in anything outside of the physical world. The magic is gone. Life is dull and has no meaning. You have become a flatlander, unable to go to higher ground to see and experience the vastness of Creation. You may be in a dead-end job, an unfulfilling relationship, and endless cycles of unfulfilling experiences. Conversely, you may be stuck in lust for your physical world, a hoarder, an addict, constantly seeking another experience, even a high adrenaline experience. At every turn, you look within every physical experience for some fulfillment, that ultimately is finite.

When caught in the shadows, it is time to turn to the light of higher consciousness and the spark of life within every creature. Most of all, it is time to look within.

The Center of the Medicine Wheel is the Place of Great Spirit

Great Spirit can be found in all life, every direction, every element. In a Medicine Wheel, Great Spirit is honored as the center of the wheel. Within the Medicine Wheel of your life, the center is at your heart space. In this way, you are always the center of the cosmos, the center of all Creation, with Great Spirit residing within you.

Totems of Great Spirit

All totems carry messages from Great Spirit and bring reminders of truth and love. Many recognize Eagle as a symbol of wisdom and higher sight for both Great Spirit and Father Sky. Always notice who shows up in your world as you pray, ask for guidance and wisdom. Honor their messages and symbolism, in addition to their synchronicity and timing. These are the reflections of Great Spirit's loving guidance.

Sounds of Great Spirit

Every creature on this planet sings the sound of Great Spirit, whether the melody of the songbird or the laughter of a child. Yet, what is recognized to be the primordial sound of the Universe according to the shamanic Hindu and Buddhist traditions is the Sanskrit word Om, or Aum. This sound represents the original seed sound of Creation. From this seed sound, all other sounds and vibrations emanate and express. From these sounds come beautiful songs of Creation, vibrating consciousness into various intricate patterns that create form.

Honoring Great Spirit as Your Ally

Great Spirit, as any ally, is to be addressed with love, gratitude, and respect, honoring the endless creative energies Great Spirit offers you. Imagine any prayer you would offer to any of the allies you can say to Great Spirit. All the various allies of the Medicine Wheel — the directions, the elements, the associated totems, or any other guides and helpers — are all unique and powerful extensions of Great Spirit.

Honor Great Spirit as the Ultimate
Expression of Unconditional, Divine Love and Truth

Great Spirit calls us to awaken in the Ceremony of Life. As mentioned earlier, the story of White Buffalo Calf Woman reminds us that all life is sacred. As a beautiful Divine Feminine emanation of Great Spirit, White Buffalo Calf Woman directs us to purify ourselves of all thoughts, beliefs, feelings, and experiences that separate us from love, belonging, unity, and the preciousness of life. She reminds us that life is a sacred ceremony and gives us directives for living in unity with all life and the love of Great Spirit.

Choose practices and rituals to purify your mental, emotional, spiritual, and physical bodies. Commit to small actions individually. This supports the whole, adding up collectively. And when possible, join together with others of like heart, in benefit for the good of the whole, and you will receive the blessings in return beyond anything you can imagine.

◊Daily Notes to Self:

Prayers and Reflections with Great Spirit

© Katherine Skaggs

Praying with Great Spirit

Pray. Be still. Look around you and look for the beauty. Honor yourself. Honor your kin. And you will find your way to honoring Great Spirit. Call to Great Spirit through the earnestness of your heart and know that your prayers are always answered. Have faith. You are surrounded and never alone. Great Spirit will find a way to show you this love each and every day if you are open and willing.

Here is an example of a Great Spirit Prayer:

Hello Great Spirit. Thank you for this dream of life! Thank you for all that you have given me, so I may dream my life with the power of a Creator. Thank you for the powers of curiosity and wonderment, and the very essence of all life being You. I hear your voice in the winds, and see your beauty in the mountains and the streams. I know you are all around me, and most of all within me. As one of your many children, I ask for your beauty, strength, and wisdom to continue to awaken my heart and my mind, that I may love more deeply, that I may see clearly your essence in all life.

Cosmic Christ
Katherine Skaggs © 2005

Guidance from Great Spirit and Great Mystery

If you truly want to hear the voice of Great Spirit and to know the Great Mystery of Creation, commit your focus inward. Deepen your shamanic practices with prayer, smudging, and shamanic journeywork, in repeated and unwavering actions. It is only through experience that you will directly know the vastness of Great Spirit around you and within you. You can read what I write or what another person writes about their experiences, but you will only 'know' if you try these things.

Choose three shamanic practices you can add to your daily routines, just as you take or vitamins or brush your teeth. Then commit to working them. With practice, you will deepen your knowledge of Great Spirit and your own Self, that you may live in balance and harmony.

Altar Work with Great Spirit
Connecting to All That IS

- ~ Choose a time for a ceremony with Great Spirit when you can step outside of linear time into no-time.
- ~ Add flowers to your altar, right in the center of everything. Choose the most beautiful and fragrant flowers that bring you great pleasure through their beauty and smell.
- ~ Light a candle in each of the four directions.
- ~ Smudge yourself and your space.
- ~ Set a sacred space where all your allies and helpers can show up to assist you.
- ~ Honor all the directions, in addition to Father Sky and Mother Earth, the ancestors, and your allies.
- ~ Drop a grounding cord into Mother Earth, and one into Father Sky.
- ~ Then say hello to Great Spirit. Set your intention to connect.
- ~ Focus on opening your heart and your spirit to Divine Creator.
- ~ Play your drum, or drum music, so that you may relax and drop into a journey space.
- ~ Still yourself by listening to the repetitive drumbeat, tuning your heart, mind, and body to the energy of Great Spirit and to the energy of complete love and acceptance.
- ~ Be in the stillness with your focus on Great Spirit, gratitude, and blessings.
- ~ When you feel complete, breathe yourself completely back into your body and into the present time.
- ~ Run your breath from crown to toe, breathing deeply in, crown to toe, to return complete and whole.
- ~ Feel the fullness of energy in your body, as well as your energy bodies.
- ~ Journal your awareness.

Jungle Dreams
Katherine Skaggs © 2009

Glossary

There are many common terms and concepts you will find throughout the world of shamanism around the globe. Many of them are used throughout this book and can be found in the Glossary to assist you in becoming more familiar.

Ally – (Spirit ally) A spiritual helper and guide who brings support and assistance. Higher-dimensional heavenly beings such as an angel, archangel, ascended master, a being from the Star Nation; an Earth realm being such as an animal, bird, insect, reptile, elemental, or fairy; or an ancestor. Be open to your allies, as they can come in many forms.

Animal Spirit Beings – Every animal (often known as spirit animals, totem animals, and power animals) has its own consciousness and energy signature. It is unique with its own symbol system and teachings.

Angels – A heavenly being of light, a spiritual guide, who is here to assist you and guide you.

Artist Shaman Self – (Inner Artist) The Divine creative aspect of your inner Self.

Ascended Master – A spiritually enlightened being who in past incarnations as an ordinary human has gone through a series of spiritual initiations to 'wake up' (such as with a Christ or Buddha.)

Ancestors – Those who have walked before us who now live in the world of Spirit.

Awakened – (Enlightened) A soul who has gone through many initiations and transformations to become spiritually aware.

Dreamtime – The place within where all possibilities and potential exist. Concurrent to the Great Void.

Earth Walk – The soul's adventure to find the deep meaning and wisdom of Spirit within the dualistic world of human experience.

Enlightened – A soul who has gone through many initiations and transformations to become spiritually aware.

False Personality – The small self, or ego-based self that is separate from its larger spiritual Self.

Father Sky – The Divine Masculine principle; the heavenly realms; the spiritual Central Sun behind our physical sun. Father Sky gives the sun, the rain, and the light required to nourish all of Mother Earth. Together we have a container to experience life in form.

Great Spirit – The Universal spiritual force of creation also known as the Divine; the Creator; Creation; the Supreme Being; the Godhead; Spirit; Wakan Tanka; the Great Mystery; and chief deity recognized in Native American tribes, as well as other cultures around the world by various names.

Great Void – (Great Cosmic Womb) The space of emptiness, the nothingness, the formlessness of possibility and potential, the creative mind substance of Akasha. The place where all seeds of desire are planted before they begin to form.

Healer Shaman Self – (Inner Healer) The transformative aspect of your inner Self, completely aligned with love, truth, compassion, and Divine Law. This is the shapeshifter within that can alchemically transform life's experiences into wisdom and harmony.

Hollow Bone – (Hollow reed) One who acts as a humble, unselfish and holy conduit, or vessel for the light and energy of Great Spirit to overflow through into the world around you, in service to Great Spirit and the greater good of all. To become a hollow bone, one must empty themselves of all false personality/ego, of all Hucha, and all separation. You must love and respect everyone, be of service to others, live in alignment with Divine Law, and keep your life in order in doing so. You are a committed spiritual helper to others and to Great Spirit, with zero self-interest for power.

Hucha – The negative, lower vibrational man-made energies of fear and trauma. Expressed as anger, envy, greed, hatred, selfishness, betrayal, judgment, injustice, power over others, to name a few.

INITIATION – The cycle of transformation from one level of spiritual understanding to a new, higher level of understanding and embodiment.

MEDICINE BAG – A small or large bag holding objects of spiritual power and meaning (shamanic medicine). May be worn or carried. Typically contains stones, sacred herbs, fur or bone of your spirit allies, and symbols of spiritual power.

MEDICINE BUNDLE – (known as a Mesa in the Andean Q'ero tradition) Like a medicine bag, a bundle, made with a sacred cloth filled with items of spiritual power and meaning (shamanic medicine). Typically contains stones, sacred herbs, fur or bone of your spirit allies, and symbols of spiritual power. It is used for personal prayers, blessings, and healing. May be used in healing ceremonies for others if so desired.

MEDICINE WHEEL – The Wheel of Life; the Circle of Life; a physical and energetic representation of the four cardinal directions, above – Father Sky, below – Mother Earth and center – Great Spirit. Walking the Medicine Wheel teaches us about living in harmony with all of Creation.

MOTHER EARTH – The Divine feminine Mother of Creation is the living Goddess of our physical earth reality. She is our Earth Mother, Mama Gaia, the Great Mother, Pachamama. This conscious, loving Mother gives us our bodies, our earth world, our food, our shelter, and all our kin—from plants and trees, to oceans and rivers, to animals, birds, insects, fish, reptiles, and humans. She gives everything. She teaches respect and responsibility, for she manifests and reflects what we are aligned with.

PLANT SPIRIT BEINGS – Every plant has its own consciousness and energy signature. It is alive and unique with its own symbol system and teachings.

POWER OBJECT – a special item or tool with shamanic medicine, spiritual purpose, and power. Shamanic power objects are created with intention and prayer. They are imbued with great healing powers that become supernatural. The 'spirit' of the power object is conscious, alive, and of service to the shaman or shamanic practitioner.

PSYCHOPOMP – A spiritual guide who helps departed spirits from their earth dream to the Spirit world, aka afterlife.

SAGE SHAMAN SELF – (Inner Sage) The wise aspect of our inner Self that arises through the tempering process of life, through deep introspection and transformative, spiritual integration. The Sage carries the powers of the Storyteller as well as the Sacred Clown.

SACRED CLOWN – (Heyoka and Contrary) This sacred aspect of the wise Sage shaman self is the enlightened contrary, the satirist, and the court jester who speaks and moves in a fashion contrary to the seriousness of the leaders of the tribe, and the ego-based false personality. This sacred one arrives when it is time to 'Lighten Up' and get over one's serious sense of self. Through unconventionality and backward ways, she acts as both a mirror and a teacher. She uses extreme behaviors to mirror unconscious attitudes, forcing you to examine your actions, doubts, fears, and beliefs. She provokes laughter in the most difficult circumstances, breaking away the pain of the situation and lifting the spirits of those involved so that they may shift and heal. If the Sacred Clown has appeared to you, know that she here to help you stop taking yourself so seriously.

SAMI – (Chi, prana, life-force.) The life-giving energies of the natural world, i.e., the powers of the Cosmos that come through the sun, the moon, the stars, and all of the planetary systems; and the energy that expresses through Mother Earth's animals, plants, the trees, the oceans, rivers, waterfalls, mountains, valleys, deserts, and soils. Everything of the natural world

SHAMANIC DEATH (and dismemberment) – The spiritual process (initiation) to completely purge an old way of being, an old identity, to be reborn into a new and higher spiritual awareness.

SHAMANIC JOURNEY – An altered or expanded state of consciousness or trance state similar to a night dream state. Within this state, the shaman or practitioner may gain spiritual guidance, direction, and healing. To access this state of expanded consciousness, use the repetitive percussive sound of the drum or rattle, trance dance, and shamanic art-making.

SHAMANIC MEDICINE – Spiritual power, consciousness, and energy providing power, guidance, protection, and support. This spiritual power resides within your very being, as well as in all of the cosmos and earth, all of the natural world (animal, bird, insect, reptile, plant, stone, mountain, valley, land, river, ocean, stream, pond, etc.) This shamanic medicine can be imbued into any item of importance, such as a piece of artwork, necklace, statuette, or sacred writing, through your intention.

SHAMAN SELF – (Inner Shaman) The illuminated aspect of the inner Self that is not constrained by fear or limited perspectives of the human experience. Rather this is the part of you that is sourced completely to the Divine.

SPIRIT GUIDE – a spiritual helper or teacher that manifests in various forms, such as an angel, archangel, ascended master, spirit animal, or ancestor. Each guide has specific powers, gifts, and personal symbol system. She brings messages, guidance, and protection.

STONE SPIRIT BEINGS – Every stone, rock, and crystal formation have its own consciousness and energy signature. It is alive and unique with its own symbol system and teachings.

STORYTELLER – An aspect of the wise, Sage inner self, who can extract the wisdom of life's experiences into fantastic stories and mythologies that teach the spiritual meaning of life.

SOUL LOSS – Fragmentation and loss of energy and aspects of the soul self, due to an accident, event, spoken words, and emotional energies that are of fear, trauma, or fright.

SOUL RETRIEVAL – The shamanic restoration process of the soul. A process of clearing trauma and fright, creating a safe place for the lost soul parts and energies to return home.

TOTEM ANIMAL – A specific spiritual helper, guide, and teacher who manifests in animal form, in the physical or in visions, with its own powers and shamanic medicine to assist you. Totem animals bring guidance, wisdom, and protection.

VISION QUEST – A vision quest is a time when you step away from your everyday life, going into the sacred inner space of silence, disconnected from the linear world, fully focused on the guidance of Spirit. A vision quest is a ritual initiation into a new cycle of purposeful life.

KATHERINE SKAGGS

Katherine Skaggs

Katherine Skaggs was born in Oklahoma in a conservative, mid-western setting where she knew at an young age that she didn't quite fit in. Although her artistic talent was recognized early on, she was still encouraged to follow more traditional paths, so she earned a BS with a teaching degree and minor in art.

As a natural empath, a seeker of Truth, and a gifted creative, Katherine found the traditional life path ultimately became the motivation to seek healing and spiritual answers that she could not find within her inherited religion.

Katherine was restless to follow her true desires to become an artist, so she returned to art school at Kansas City Art Institute at age 26 and earned a Bachelor of Fine Arts in painting. This change in location and environment also allowed her to synchronistically discover the study of metaphysics, dreams, past lives, and all things spiritual.

Just a few years later, Katherine became both a teacher and the *Director of Schools* for a nationally known school of metaphysics. Then, in her early 30s, she founded a metaphysical retail store and learning center where she also taught and facilitated a conscious community.

Katherine began her path in the multi-cultural world of shamanism during her 40s for personal healing. During these studies Katherine completed an advanced international two-year program in shamanism, which began her journeys to study with shamans in Peru and Mexico. She went on to continue these studies with Shipibo shamans in the jungles of Peru, the Q'ero shamans in the high Andes, and the Huichol shamans in Central Mexico. She ultimately continued along this path to become a shamanic practitioner, teacher, and ceremonialist.

Katherine lives and works as a visionary artist, writer, intuitive channel, spiritual teacher and guide, shamanic practitioner, and soul portrait painter. She is the artist of the <u>Mythical Goddess Tarot Deck</u> and several mini-decks. She's created more than 90 inspirational Altar Cards born of her acclaimed, contemplative art and inspired writing.

Katherine has painted thousands of Soul Portraits and Spirit Guide Paintings helping others to connect more deeply with their inner-selves, heal, and see their beauty.

The <u>Artist Shaman Healer Sage</u> book is born of Katherine's exploration of creativity, spirituality, and shamanism. She has woven together priceless teachings through the unique insights of her direct mystical experiences and her own awakenings.

www.KatherineSkaggs.com

An Invitation

Change the World - Gather in Circles

Share What you Learn, Remotely or In-Person

The wisdom and practices found within <u>Artist Shaman Healer Sage</u> are a potent way to restore harmony and balance within oneself, as well as throughout your world. As *you* receive the blessing of self-transformation with these teachings, you are encouraged to share your growth with others, in ways that are meaningful to you.

You may discover people you already know have an interest in this method of wisdom journey. I've found the best way to share in the teachings and practices is with humility and openness.

Gather with one, with several, with many. Open a Circle or Medicine Wheel that will embrace you in ceremony, ritual, and wisdom teachings. Reflect on what you are learning through direct experience, transcending the mental into a full embodiment of the practices and principles.

You are the change in the world that you desire. Gathering in sacred circles with clarity of intention, humility, and openness is an exponential way to create change.

Let Me Support You in Supporting Your Community

If you are a teacher, coach, or leader who facilitates gatherings and you are interested in using this book as a guide, please contact me for quantity discounts.

With much love and many blessings,

Katherine Skaggs